POWER and *Soul*

42 Successful Entrepreneurs Share Their Secrets for
Creating the Business and Life
of Your Dreams

COMPILED BY ALEXANDRIA K. BROWN

Published by Love Your Life
PO Box 2, Dallastown, PA 17313

Copyright © 2007

Published in the US and Canada by Love Your Life

ISBN 10: 0-9664806-8-6
ISBN 13: 978-0-9664806-8-9

Library of Congress Control No: 2004097825

www.LoveYourLife.com
(717) 200-2852

SAN 256-1387

Book Design by Cyanotype Book Architects

This book is dedicated to the amazing members
*of my **Marketing & Motivation Mastermind**,*
who inspire me daily…
and bring me more joy than any other pursuit
I've taken on in my life.

Love and Success,

ALEXANDRIA K. BROWN

❧ Contents

Part II: Turning Your Dreams Into Reality

Part IV: From Surviving to Thriving

⁓ INTRODUCTION

by Alexandria K. Brown

You may not know my name, or those of the 42 amazing entrepreneurs in this book who are from around the world, but you're about to know our stories. And I believe our words will stay with you for a long time to come.

Most of the authors in this book started from less-than-nothing and faced unimaginable hardships and challenges in the past. But they had a dream. And in this book I asked them to share the biggest lessons they learned on the way to the top. These are stories about wealth, purpose, courage, health, family, personal power, and passion for life. You'll find within they share gems of advice on a wide variety of topics.

But I hope one of the most profound things that stands out in your mind as you read *Power and Soul* is that, while all of our journeys were unique, how striking it is that we all ultimately arrived at success by finding the power within us.

Besides having some amazing stories to share, these authors are also all part of my Marketing & Motivation Mastermind, which says a lot about them. It shows they take responsibility for their success, they value ongoing education and support, and they greatly understand the value of investing in themselves. (If you'd like to learn more about joining this stellar group of entrepreneurs, see the back of this book.)

When I announced the *Power and Soul* project to my Mastermind members in the fall of 2006, the authors in this book are the ones who jumped at the opportunity to share their lives with you. Some of them, as you'll read, had the courage to be very vulnerable with you in the following chapters. They share their early hardships, the tough lessons they've learned, the challenges they met along their own personal journeys. And they generously also give us the steps they took to course-correct, reach for the top, and even surpass their expectations.

Success is never achieved by walking a straight path. It's most often a curvy, twisty, bumpy, and exciting road. But we wouldn't change it for the world! Our stories come together like pieces of a puzzle to reveal: We would not have found our *Power and Soul* without these unique journeys that were presented to us.

As you read through *Power and Soul,* you'll be likely to find there are a few select chapters that seemed as if they were written personally for YOU. These are the ones to pay special attention to, because you attracted this book into your hands to receive that specific message.

Read and enjoy. And I wish you Power and Soul.

Love and Success,

Alexandria K. Brown

PART I

Power Strategies for Business Success

CHAPTER I

Dreams Come True (and It's Easier Than You Think): The 3 Keys to How I Built a Million-Dollar Home Business

ALEXANDRIA K. BROWN

I'm writing this sitting in my new, giant, cushy, white easy-chair I call the "marshmallow," watching the sun set over the Pacific Ocean through my 15-foot glass doors. My cat Francine is by my side and we're watching the sky change colors over the water and sand, from blue and pink to orange and purple. My palm tree on the patio is gently swaying in the ocean breeze. I'm surrounded by luxurious furniture, and there's relaxing lounge music piping through my entire house in the background. On the table in front of me is paperwork for the third 10-day tropical vacation I'll take this year, featuring first class air tickets and luxury accommodations.

I take a sip of my chilled Pinot Grigio and think… it's moments like this I have to pinch myself. It's an unbelievable feeling, when you've been struggling so hard for so long (and you thought it had to be that way), and then suddenly… the system appears, the dam is broken, the money is flowing in like a river from the heavens. I now understand there is indeed a universal flow of abundance.

But if you'd told me 8 years ago that I'd be living in a $1.3 million beach house, working from home on my own easy schedule, money coming in day and night via my website, looking and feeling better than I ever have in my life, being debt-free, giving tens of thousands of dollars to charities each year, and creating this dream lifestyle as a single girl, I'd say "I think you have me mixed up with somebody else!"

You see, things were very different back then.

In fact, just the other day I had a terrible flashback to the year I started my first business. It was a cold, rainy night in New York City, and I was running late to meet some friends for a drink. My spirits were already sour as I learned earlier that day that all 5 credit cards I owned were maxed out, and I was very worried about my financial situation. I had a few clients I was writing and consulting for, but there was no consistent, reliable income.

I went to the ATM and requested $20. The ATM churned a bit, and then… I'll never forget that ugly green screen flashing… "Transaction Denied: Insufficient Funds".

Yes folks, I had $18.56 to my name. (My stomach knots up even as I write this.)

In shock, I took back my card, called my friends, said something came up and I was sorry but I'd be unable to meet up with them. I walked back home, trudged up the five flights of stairs to my tiny pre-war 400-square-foot apartment, pulled my Murphy Bed down from the wall, got in under the blankets with my suit still on, curled up in a ball, and cried.

Having no money hurt. But it hurt even more because I was really trying so hard! Working relentlessly, day after day, doing all the things I thought you were supposed to do when you owned a business. I worked like a dog, jumped for my clients, networked like crazy all over the city, and took no time for anything so "trivial" like exercise or sleep. I was giving it my all. And I still had no money, time, or freedom.

I had started my business because I wanted to control my own destiny. But now, my business owned me. And it was a masochistic affair.

Something had to change. This was too HARD.

But wasn't that how it's supposed to be? I mean, it can't be easy.

Wait…

Or can it?

Well, I have a secret to share with you…

I know now it CAN be easy. It can be fun. And it can be more financially and personally rewarding than you ever thought possible. This year my business has already surpassed $1,000,000.00 in revenues.

Yes… *one million dollars!*

So what did I do over the last few years to turn my life around so dramatically? MANY things, most of which I teach now via my workshops and coaching programs, but here are three of the most important that you can use right away:

1. STOP WORKING HOURS-FOR-DOLLARS.

Ah, the real nuts-and-bolts of how I catapulted my income, time, and freedom. You will never become wealthy by working hours for dollars. Why? Even if you charge a lot, you are still limited to the number of hours you want to work.

You need to instead learn how to leverage your current assets. (And don't worry; you don't need money as an asset to get started.)

The good news is you also don't need to change your current business or area of specialty. All you need to do is change your business *model*. In my case, I shifted from an "hours for dollars" business model to one that leverages my knowledge and expertise—not my time.

Information marketing is a business model that does not drain me, but instead excites me, helps thousands more people, brings in much more income, and gives me tons more free time. And I'm still using the same knowledge and expertise I was using in my former business.

I work no more than 8 hours a day and an average of 4 days a week. I'm also not chained to my phone or email—I refuse to get one of those Blackberry things! In fact, I can go away on a two-week vacation and my business will run itself while I'm gone, bringing money in all the while.

And what's great is *anyone* can make this shift! The exact steps involved are what I now teach via my live Online Success Blueprint™ Workshops; my Platinum, Gold, and Silver Mastermind programs; and my assorted home study programs.

2. Accept that your success can be EASY. (It just takes work.)

Ha ha, yes, that irony was intended. I was disappointed to learn earlier in my life that many Bible-based teachings condone working until the point of exhaustion, and claim that is how you earn blessings and prosperity. We're conditioned to think it has to be a hard struggle to "earn" our riches. But success does not come about from simply working hard. There are ditch diggers who work very hard—"harder" than you and I both—but they will never become wealthy.

Your true success will come from working SMART—learning exactly what strategies will make you the most money and bring you the most fulfillment, and ignoring all the rest. Then, focusing on the simplest, easiest ways to attract the success you desire *faster*. These are very simple principles, but as with most things worth doing, they are easier said than done. There are many steps involved, and that's why I spend so much time teaching this subject. And it's extremely rewarding. Once my coaching students get these ideas down, it's amazing how fast the changes come, almost effortlessly!

3. Stop caring what others think, step up, and SHINE.

I recently saw a statistic that revealed only 6% of people in the United States make over $100,000 a year. That means, when it comes to making money, 94% of the country has their heads up their you-know-whats. But who do we grow up learning to model? Yep, that 94%. We go to school to learn to be like them, and then graduate looking for jobs to be like them. Then we live our lives like them and wonder why we get the same results as them.

This is exactly why your friends and family (the ones in that 94%), will look at you crookedly for wanting more. For having higher standards. For willing (and expecting), to be different. For refusing to accept a life less than extraordinary, AND for being 100% willing to risk everything to go after it.

Whenever I'd get the "who does she think she is" looks and comments from colleagues (and yes, it still happens), I would re-read this powerful quote by Marianne Williamson:

> "Our deepest fear is not that we are inadequate. Our deepest fear is that we are powerful beyond measure. It is our light, not our darkness that most frightens us. We ask ourselves, Who am I to be brilliant, gorgeous, talented, fabulous? Actually, who are you not to be? You are a child of God. Your playing small does not serve the world. There is nothing enlightened about shrinking so that other people won't feel insecure around you… And as we let our own light shine, we unconsciously give other people permission to do the same…."

Your job is to stand tall, be your best self, and work for *your* highest good. That in itself will attract more success into your life (and the lives of others), than you'd ever imagined.

About the Author:

Online entrepreneur **Alexandria K. Brown** *publishes the award-winning* Straight Shooter Marketing *weekly ezine with over 21,000 subscribers. Her* Mastermind Coaching Programs, Online Success Blueprint™ Workshops, *and home-study materials have helped thousands of solopreneurs just like you jump-start their marketing, make a lot more money, work less, and have tons more fun in their businesses. Don't wait any longer—get your hands on all Ali's FREE tips, articles, and audio classes at* www.AlexandriaBrown.com.

CHAPTER 2

How to Put the Universal Law of Attraction to Work in Your Business

Toni O'Bryan

Nourishing Your Greatest Asset

Running a business can seem like a juggling act. Business, after all, is about managing assets. Product is an essential asset, of course, but every day you're challenged by other assets that demand your attention. You need to inspire and motivate your staff every day. You know that branding isn't just a logo, but every element of your business; from the organic beverage you serve at meetings to the way you answer the phone. Unless you've recently won the lottery (and if you have, call me!), you're constantly reading and questioning your financial reports… but those assets aren't what I'm referring to.

Your most important asset—far more important and far more valuable—should be your highest priority. It will help you achieve what every business is in business for: to earn a higher return on investment.

Your greatest asset—that which you should focus on above all others—is your life force. Your energy.

Breaking the Law

I began my career in graphic design with tons of energy. I was fast, efficient and determined in my pursuit of success. I didn't sleep as much as I should and many times I ate at my desk to save time. I was in a competitive, deadline-driven field and was considered quite successful, with awards in my bookcase, respect from my peers and a portfolio to die for.

Until I nearly died. All this time, I thought the stress and anxiety I'd been feeling somehow fueled my energy. Quite the opposite! I started getting sick and weak for no apparent reason until I was diagnosed with Chronic Fatigue Syndrome (CFS).

There's no pill to cure CFS. No magic elixir. No treatment.

I came to learn that I'd been breaking the Law. A universal Law. And my life, not to mention my success, depended on obeying the Universal Law of Attraction.

Obeying the Law

Faced with CFS, I had to un-learn all of the energy-draining habits and patterning that I had created around me. Luckily, I was led to energetic healing work and modalities that affect the subconscious mind. I started obeying the Law of Attraction. Two or three times a day, I spent time in meditation and found alternative methods to help focus my attention on the perfect health and lifestyle I wanted. I listened to tapes, read, danced more, did everything I could to raise my energy level.

In less than two years, I conquered CFS and have enjoyed excellent health since. If I can turn that mess around, you too can surely create a successful business life that works for you.

The Law

By now, you've probably heard about the Universal Law of Attraction. You may have seen the movies *The Secret*, *What The Bleep*, read

Abraham-Hicks' book *Ask and It's Given,* or have stumbled upon it through a conscious business organization or expo. If you haven't, you may be surprised at how simple it is. The Law of Attraction states, "like attracts like". Whatever you focus on the most is what will be most attracted to you. You are a living, breathing magnet.

Everybody and everything is made up of energy. Every thought, feeling and action requires energy. Everything surrounding you and your environment is energy. $E=mc^2$. The furniture, the people, the sounds, and the earth itself. Energy is set to a vibratory rate, and everything you come in contact with is either increasing or decreasing your individual power.

The beautiful thing about the Law of Attraction is that it ALWAYS WORKS. The Law of Attraction is not some new age trend it is scientific fact. It is one of the basic principles of life and has been around since creation. Just like gravity, the Law of Attraction works whether you know it, believe it, understand it or not.

Everything in your business is a result of what you were focusing on the most in the past—nothing is exempt. We're responsible for all of it. This includes what we want and what we don't want. Yes, that includes the client that you can't find when payments are due—and the always empty roll of toilet paper.

STRATEGIES FOR USING THE LAW

There are three simple steps according to Abraham-Hicks:

Step 1: Ask.
Step 2: It is given.
Step 3: Allow yourself to receive.

Step 1: When asking, clarity is the key. The more clarity you have, the stronger, and clearer signal you'll be sending out. This applies to business very easily.

- Before making a call or writing a letter to a client or potential client, take a second. Be clear of your intended results. Take a deep breath and visualize it, what it looks like, feels like. Focus on the details. Say it, write it down, draw it.
- In the branding process, you will gain greater clarity by asking questions at the onset such as: Who is your ideal client? Why are you the best at what you do? Why do you do it?
- When sending out a marketing piece, first get clear on what your intention is for that piece. What do you want the result to be for the receiver—and for you?

Step 2: Easy. This one is out of your hands. It is automatically given.

Step 3: To receive it, you must be vibrationally aligned with it. You must do everything at first to feel good. Treat yourself. Do this throughout the day, every day.

Allow this to happen. Don't focus on the fact that it hasn't arrived. You'll create more of "it hasn't arrived" and delay its materialization. Focus only on what you want to create, not what you don't.

When thinking about your creation, see it in present time, feel how good it feels to have it—sense it—KNOW IT.

In our studio, we're fascinated with ritual and spiritual practices from around the world. They do a lot to keep the energy and focus of our studio on track. Here are a few simple suggestions:

- begin by setting an intention for the day: again, see it, feel it
- light a candle
- set intentions before meetings
- drink a ceremonial tea
- hug co-workers
- use sacred aromatherapy tinctures
- dance breaks
- play high vibrational music
- yogic breathing or stretching breaks
- hold the Egyptian Healing Rods

- play a healing sound instrument e.g. tingshaws, crystal bowls
- post reminders and inspirational sayings on computer screens
- read gratitude lists
- laugh real loud

Nothing nourishes your asset like a good laugh. The energy of joy and laughter is at a very high vibration. According to Dr. David Hawkin's decades of research, the vibration of the emotional state of joy is at the level of 540. Compare this with Guilt which is at 30, Fear at 100, Acceptance at 350, and Enlightenment, which is around 700-1000.

- Schedule appointments for fun. This aspect is vitally important to the success of your business. Fun companies attract fun clients.
- Bring pets to work.
- Have a joke of the day.

We've added another step.

Step 4: Celebrate!
Celebrate the matches to what you've been creating. The energy of celebration could just be the extra boost you need to be at that PERFECT MATCHING VIBRATION of your desire. When you are seeing a result of your creation, even if it's not exact, celebrate it! Honor it Document it Jump up and down. Throw a party!

LEVERAGING THE PROCESS

According to Abraham-Hicks, a thought reaches a combustion point at 17 seconds of pure undiluted focus. If you can continue a pure thought for 68 seconds on any given subject, it will be on its way to manifestation. The key word is PURE. This means positive focus, strong energy, no resistance.

Just 17 seconds is worth 2,000 man hours (about a year, at 40 hours per week of action taken).

The average person rarely finishes a single sentence without contradicting their energy, as in "I want a new car, but it is too expensive." They say most of us haven't had much experience with ever feeling the combustion of thought that comes from 17+ seconds of pure thought.

ACCELERATING THE PROCESS

- Make room for your creation. Clear the physical space for it. Make room for more client folders—room for growth.
- Read your desire every day.
- Remember to laugh.
- See your words as beautiful white creative light, connecting to white light of your creation and bringing it to you.
- Trust that it will come. Doubting slows it down.
- Always focus on what you DO want.
- Remember every thought carries an energy vibration. Thoughts can be measured.
- Plan fun into your work schedule.
- Clear the blockages—mental, emotional, spiritual.
- Express gratitude and love for what you already have.

PUTTING IT TO WORK RIGHT NOW

Why wait? Let's create something right now!

About the Author:

Toni O'Bryan's *company* KaChing! *brings spiritual principles into the brands they create. She works with leading edge entrepreneurs that have socially, environmentally and spiritually-based businesses. As an Award-winning Brand Consultant, Graphic Designer, Marketer, Avesa Quantum Healer™ and Self Ascension Coach, she uses powerful healing processes, tools and resources so they can transform themselves AND their businesses. Visit* www.kaching-creative.com *for a free report* 5 Secrets to A Prospering Conscious Business. *Email* toni@kaching-creative.com *or call Toni at 310-581-9007.*

CHAPTER 3

C'mon Girl—
It's Time To Throw Your Girdle
Into Your Business!

KIM DUKE

I am a huge fan of Great DAMES.

Women who were gutsy determined, and who were willing to take risks to get ahead.

Years ago I stumbled across a television documentary that profiled a woman who absolutely BLEW MY MIND with her drive, amazing accomplishments and also her sense of fun.

She was a woman many of you have probably never heard of.

Her name is Babe Zaharias—who was once called "the athletic phenomenon of all time, man or woman."

She played basketball; set world records at hurdles; javelin and high jump, and struck gold twice at the 1932 Olympics. She next went on to transform women's golf with her 250 yard drive and she became a tennis champion—winning the US Open 3 times.

Hard to believe (but true!), in her spare time she also became a pro billiard player.

In a time when most women were carrying a broom, Babe Zaharias was carrying a golf club.

She said something so powerful that I have it posted directly over my desk—as a constant reminder…

"It's not just enough to swing at the ball. You've got to loosen your girdle and REALLY let the ball have it."

Are You Just Swinging At The Ball or Are You Really Loosening Your Girdle?

So many women entrepreneurs I meet in my travels ask me this question:

"What do I need to do to be successful in selling?"

It all comes down to being willing to ask yourself a tough question.

Are you just swinging at the ball—or are you loosening up your girdle and really being DARING and DIFFERENT—PASSIONATE and PERSISTENT?

This is something I ask myself on a daily basis as I know what you FOCUS ON EXPANDS.

The BIGGEST Sales Mistake!

The biggest mistake in selling is also the most DANGEROUS.

Why is it dangerous?

It is something that may be currently squeezing the LIFE out of your business and MONEY out of your bank account.

What is the mistake?

Being Boring Beyond Belief!

The bold Katharine Hepburn said it best.

"If you're not standing out—then you are blending in with the wallpaper."

The temptation in business is to want to be just like your competition. But then you are blending with the wallpaper! (and your customer doesn't have a compelling reason to CHOOSE YOU.)

Years ago I remember seeing a cheesy motel sign that said "TV. Carpet. Air Conditioning."

I laughed out loud!

Now… I am not sure about you, but when I am looking for a place to stay, I EXPECT THESE THINGS. (Carpet? Are they kidding me??) They aren't exceptional—they are expected!

Why Is it Important To Be Daring and Different?

I worked for years in the media in sales and management. One of the most important points I stressed to my clients is that there is nothing beautiful or advantageous about being "vanilla."

Your customer/potential customer is searching for someone who can solve their problems in a creative manner.

If you base your business i.e. advertising, marketing, product etc. on what your COMPETITION is doing, then you have entered the world of vanilla where you are blending in, baby!

EXPECTING AND EXPERIENCING— Some Diva Secrets!

Ask yourself these 2 questions:

What does my customer EXPECT from my company?

How can I elevate the EXPERIENCE for them?

3. Unusual "Girdle" Tips To Set Yourself Apart

1. Be Contrary

Ask yourself—How can I position myself as DIFFERENT?

Customers don't need more ordinary—they need more of the Extraordinary…and the beautiful part is that simple activities (done consistently), will set you apart!

- Review your business—What can be revised 1-10% that

would THRILL your customer? (Send out personal thank you cards, include something fun in your invoice etc.)

2. Find the Gaps

Some of the most interesting opportunities come from the areas where NEEDS AREN'T BEING MET.

When I first decided to become an entrepreneur I knew that most people were afraid to death of selling. They wanted to have their own successful business and yet they were terrified of how to ask customers for money.

I realized that KNOWING HOW TO SELL was a huge gap that my potential customers needed, and that I could fill that GAP by showing them the best way to do it. And so The Sales Divas was born.

An interesting example of finding a GAP is a recent blog I discovered.

One of the most unique blogs that is gaining international attention is http://postsecret.blogspot.com/

People send in their anonymous secrets on an actual postcard.

Why is it unique? People are searching for a "safe confessional" and being creative at the same time. The postcards are now available in a huge book at major bookstores!

Realize that it is important to look at your business from every possible angle (even upside down!), to see the GAPS that could become incredible revenue streams for you.

3. WHAT Are You Doing Wrong?

I love Einstein. (Sometimes we even share the same hair style!)

His quote *"Within every problem resides a glorious opportunity"* has always put a huge grin on my face.

I love finding opportunities where others see problems!

Last year I was in Los Angeles attending a convention at an airport hotel.

What's the problem with an airport hotel?

Planes. Planes. Planes. Flying at all hours of the night over your cozy little bed.

When I first walked into the hotel room I was thinking "Oh great—another sleepless night away from home!"

And then I was pleasantly surprised!

This hotel understood what their biggest problem was. They were offering a place to sleep in an environment that doesn't promote sleep!

On the nightstand there was a little "Sleep Kit". It was incredible!

A little bottle of lavender spray, earplugs, chocolate, and a CD—guided meditation to go to sleep. There was actually a CD player in the room that wasn't chained down!

I used everything in the kit and it worked wonderfully!

They turned a potentially nasty experience into a fabulous one. And all it took was some ingenuity and a few dollars per room to create a happy customer.

You've Got To Be Passionate and Persistent!
Starting your own business requires having a backbone instead of a wishbone.

In order to succeed you are going to have to strettttttttttttttttttttttttttttt ch the boundaries i.e. the girdle of your mind and go beyond what you originally thought was possible.

My biggest piece of advice to you?

Have a vision and a passion for a business that means something to you. People who get into business to just make a quick buck will find themselves in trouble very rapidly.

Babe Zaharias was passionate about sports. I am passionate about helping women entrepreneurs succeed in selling.

What are YOU passionate about?

Persistence Is The Key!

Remember—Rome wasn't built in a day and neither was my make-up bag. You want to be a successful business owner? Then you are going to have to commit to excellence with everything that you do.

You are going to persist even when your bank account feels a little limp, or when you have had some obstacles put in your path. If you fold like a taco the first time a situation doesn't go your way, then you should probably go work for someone else.

There are 2 inspiring quotes I read when I am feeling frustrated and need clarity.

"When you are at the end of your rope—tie a knot in it and hang on!"
—Eleanor Roosevelt

"The path is clear. Why do you throw stones before you?"
—Chinese Proverb

I don't know what your situation is but I do know this.

You can change it. Again and again and again.

I think Babe Zaharias knew a few things and she definitely would have been someone I would have loved to have met. Can you imagine the insight? The drive? The wisdom?

If she could see into your mind and business right now—would she be impressed or disappointed with you?

So ask yourself today "Am I just swinging at the ball or have I REALLY put my girdle into it?"

Your business and your customers will thank you for it!

About the Author:

Kim Duke, *The Sales Diva, provides savvy, sassy sales training for women small biz owners and entrepreneurs. Kim works with clients international-ly, showing them The Sales Diva secrets to success! Sign up for her saucy and smart FREE e-zine and receive her FREE Bonus Report* The 5 Biggest Sales Mistakes Women Make *at* www.SalesDivas.com. *For speaking engagements or media interviews, contact her at 1-780-432-3903.*

CHAPTER 4

The Fastest Path to Productivity and Profit: How Implementing Systems in Your Business Will Completely Change Your Life

FABIENNE FREDRICKSON

In years of teaching entrepreneurs to attract lots of paying clients on a consistent basis, I've seen countless small business owners frustrated about marketing. Most had read the marketing books, yet were not attracting clients regularly. Many considered going back to working for someone else. Looking into their eyes, it seemed they'd been robbed of their innate power and even a bit of their spirit.

I'd been one of those people once too. Back in 1999, I'd quit my corporate job and opened up a private nutrition practice out of my home. I had gotten some great clients right away. Problem was, I didn't have enough clients to consistently pay my rent. I began to toss and turn in the middle of the night from what I now call the "3-am-I-don't-have-enough-clients-sweats." I stopped answering my phone when credit card companies started calling on a daily basis. I'd officially hit rock bottom.

As I saw it, I had two choices: 1) I could throw in the towel, accept defeat and go back to the corporate world; or 2) I'd have to figure out what it was going to take to get enough clients to always pay the bills comfortably, and have money left over to enjoy myself. Since going back to Corporate was not an option for me, I made a commitment to give it my all, as if my life depended on it (in a very real way, it did.) I took back my power and put myself, almost overnight, in a position of control over the outcome of my business. I was going to do what it would take to get clients.

I bought the sales books, took courses and learned all I could about marketing, networking, closing the sale and time management. I tried everything, and realized that a lot of it worked and a lot didn't. Some nights, I would put my head on the pillow and cry from sheer exhaustion and frustration.

After a few months, I figured out what was valid from what wasn't. Finally, it worked! Within 8 short months, I'd filled my practice to capacity, started paying down my debt, and actually enjoyed being self employed. It felt like a miracle. Along the way, I made three startling observations:

1. Marketing experts talked a good game, but a lot of the strategies either didn't work for me or weren't realistic on my shoestring budget.
2. All the marketing information I needed was not available in just one place.
3. Once I figured out what actually worked to get clients, marketing became easy and fun, especially when I created systems and put my marketing on autopilot.

So, to make sure I never experienced feast or famine again, I compiled all my strategies and techniques into a repeatable, predictable and verifiable plan that would ensure I always attracted clients, easily and consistently. I assembled all the elements into one system called The Client Attraction System™.

It worked so well that I quickly transitioned into teaching other struggling entrepreneurs the techniques I'd been applying. Soon, my business coaching practice was born and also filled to capacity in 8 months. Since then, I've taught thousands of small business owners to market themselves consistently and make more money than they've ever made before, with greater ease.

What I've discovered over the years is that having a full practice has little to do with discipline, willpower or hard work. The secret? It's all about systems for running a business so that the systems work for you (not the other way around), and that you actually enjoy your life.

After implementing the marketing steps from the Client Attraction Home Study System™, the first thing I recommend to clients is using the following techniques to work more effectively:

1. Putting a marketing plan on autopilot happens by creating a system for every single aspect of what you do to attract clients (That way, you don't have to think about what to do next, you just follow the system.)

2. Make sure your entire schedule is systematized. For me, clients get the same time slot, the same day of the week, for the entire time we work together. This saves administrative costs and lots of scheduling time.

3. Eliminate in-person meetings with people, even prospects. Whereby it took me 15 minutes to drive to an appointment, an hour or so for an in-person meeting, and 15 minutes to drive back, I now prefer to save that time and have a 15 minute phone conversation instead. It works just as well and saves time for other things that really matter.

4. All prospects calling for coaching programs get handled by my virtual staff, saving me lots of valuable time.

5. Create a Business Development Only day, so that you can work on your marketing undisturbed. Being in the "flow" allows you to be more creative.

6. Hire a professional organizer to come in several times per year to help you create systems for your paperwork. It's not expensive and

it really helps.

7. Create a Daily Breakout of what you're going to do each day, so you can fit everything that matters most, before all the non-essentials eat up all your time.

8. Have a shared calendar with your assistant (such as Groove.net), so you can delegate client scheduling entirely.

9. Schedule follow-ups in your calendar as you would a client appointment, either daily or right after a networking event.

10. Turn emails you regularly send into templates you keep in the Drafts folder of your email program (tweaking email templates instead of writing one from scratch saves an enormous amount of time each day.)

11. Use checklists for everything to streamline the time it takes to do something and to make sure nothing falls through the cracks. (We have checklists for public speaking, the publication of our weekly ezine, setting up group programs, etc.) Things run much more smoothly with these.

12. Use any and all travel time for follow up with prospects or writing articles and new programs.

13. Use the Low Hanging Fruit List for keeping track of all prospects that express interest in working with you. (I give an example of it in my home study system.) Using this procedure ensures that no prospect ever slips through your fingers again, which equals more clients and more money.

14. Color-code your Outlook calendar for easy reference (I use white/blank for client appointments, red for speaking gigs, orange for new prospect appointments, blue for networking, and green for personal appointments.)

15. Set up folders in Outlook for each category or each client, including a folder for Referrals and one for Speaking Opportunities, to help you keep track of it all.

16. Set up rules in Outlook so particular emails go to their respective folders, saving you lots of time and helping you prioritize your email. (I've set up email rules so that all my VIP client emails au-

tomatically get transferred to the VIP folder; rules for my personal emails, rules for newsletters I receive, etc.)

17. Have systems and scripts set up for closing the sale, as I do, so that the system works for you and closing the sale is much more predictable.

With a husband and two children under the age of 4, I recommend systems on the home front too: weekly online grocery shopping and delivery, weekly pickup and delivery of our dry cleaning, systems around what to make for a dinner each night, for packing the kids' lunches, regular haircuts, doctor's appointments, etc.

What I've noticed is that, whereby I used to think that systems were boring and restrictive, they create quite the opposite effect. When the systems are in place and they work hard for you, as opposed to you working hard, it affects both your business and your personal life. On the business front, fewer things fall through the cracks, things run smoothly and you have the capacity and the time to take on more clients, create more products or simply make more money.

On the home front, having systems means that you have time for what matters most. For me, that's closing my office at 5:15 to spend quality time with my children and having "date night" with my husband every night, even if it's at home, and being able to spend time by myself to really enjoy life and its richness. Without systems, I truly believe that my soul would feel less fulfilled. So, in essence, the structure I rebelled against now gives me the freedom to enjoy my life to its fullest. And for me, that's what it's all about.

Your assignment:

Make a list of everything that's falling through the cracks in your business (and even at home.) Then, look at each item on the list and create a way of systematizing the solution to the problem so that it gets handled easily, efficiently and without fail. You'll start living life with a lot more ease and start having more fun, guaranteed.

About the Author:

Fabienne Fredrickson *is founder of* The Client Attraction System™, *the most complete Client Attraction training and coaching program for entrepreneurs. Using her unique marketing principles, Fabienne went from a mediocre practice, to one bursting at the seams in less than 8 months. Fabienne is author of two manuals, both available on* www.ClientAttraction.com. *For more information, email info@clientattraction.com or call 1-866-RAINMAKER. For your free special report* How to Attract All the Clients You Need, *visit* www.ClientAttraction.com.

CHAPTER 5

The Truth About Selling—
and How It Can Make You
More Successful

ARI GALPER

This is a true story...

It happened about 6 years ago when I was doing direct selling—after having spent several years studying all the great sales gurus; designing sales training for UPS, Qualcomm, and other major companies; and finishing my master's degree in instructional design, which focuses on studying how people learn.

On that fateful afternoon, I was on the phone doing an online demonstration with the top executives of a software company.

Have you ever had a sales call that felt like a "love fest"? This one was like that. Everything was going by the book. They were interested, they were asking me tons of questions, I had all the answers at my fingertips. At the end of the call, they thanked me profusely for my time. And the vice president's final words were, "We'll definitely be getting back to you."

I was so proud of how well things had gone that I could almost feel my head swell as I started to hang up the phone.

But then...instead of pushing the phone's *off* button, I accidentally hit the *mute* button. I didn't realize it until I heard them continuing to talk. They hadn't hung up, but they thought I had.

I just had to keep listening. And what do you think they were saying about our oh-so-promising phone conversation?

"Okay…" It was the vice-president's voice. "So, we're definitely not going to go with him. But keep stringing him along. Get more information so we can get a better deal with another company."

Ouch! I was devastated…

My first feeling was outrage that they had lied to me. I felt hurt and used, but the feelings of rejection that swept over me were even worse. "I'm a good guy," I told myself. "I did everything right. I've studied all the best sales programs in the world. I didn't cut any corners. Why are they treating me this way?"

Then I remembered a lot of other times when I had gotten a gut feeling that something was "off" about how a prospect was reacting to me. I could never put my finger on it, but at some level I knew that everything I had learned was incomplete. But I ignored that nagging discomfort and kept on doing what I had been doing, until that wakeup call.

You know, a lot of sales programs today would analyze that call and say: "If a prospect lies to you, it's okay to lie back. If they're aggressive to you, it's okay to be aggressive back, because that's how you can control the situation. If they try to box you in, it's okay to force them into a commitment."

But this buyer and seller conflict… battle… whatever you want to call it… just felt so wrong.

It took me a long time to figure out one basic truth that none of those "fight-back" sales programs ever talked about:

The problem wasn't with the prospect. It was with me. There was something fundamentally wrong with how I was approaching selling. And I needed to change.

It was at this point that I was finally able to let go of the outrage and rejection and take responsibility for having tried to sell the "wrong" way.

Once I shifted my thinking from focusing on them to **focusing on what I was doing**, the answers started to come. I realized that the old ways of selling had everything backward. And that freed me to begin thinking about what ultimately became Unlock The Game.

They knew I had an agenda for that call, which was to make them buy what I had to sell. I tried to do it by going with my script, developing it, dealing with their "objections," pushing subtly to move things forward…you know the drill.

And they seemed to be playing along, and I wouldn't have known any differently if I hadn't accidentally hit the *mute* button that fateful day.

The problem was the whole dynamic of trying to make the sale.

- Did it ever occur to me to think about ways I could develop **a relationship of trust** in which we could explore what issues and problems they were trying to solve? No.
- Did I ever suggest that, without knowing more about their issues and problems, I couldn't know whether what I had to offer could help them? No.
- Did it ever occur to me to ask them, "Where do you think you might want to go from here?" No.

 I was on that call to make a sale, and the implicit sales pressure I was exerting with every word I spoke made them feel it was okay to lead me on and even lie to me.

Think about it—would they have lied to me if they trusted that I wouldn't exert sales pressure on them regardless of their decision? Probably not.

So that's really the day that Unlock The Game started to come into existence, although it took me several years to develop all the principles and ideas that are now in the Mastery Program—the Mindset and what it means, and how to express these principles in language and behavior that is gracious, low-key, respectful, and above all, **focused on the prospect** rather than the person selling.

Although that conference call was very painful, I have to say that I'm grateful that it happened. Otherwise, I would probably still be selling the old way instead of working with so many people to release the pain of selling and move into a place of trust and open communication with your prospects.

Here are some lessons I learned from that fateful conference call:

- **Rejection can only happen if you're focused on your own agenda.** Rejection happens when you go for the "yes" instead of the truth. If you focus on your prospect's issues and problems and whether your solution might be a fit for them, rejection is no longer a possibility. After all, how can rejection result from a conversation void of any hidden agendas?

- **Take a few minutes to "debrief" yourself after each call or selling encounter.** Don't just make your calls and forget about them, because every call can be an important learning experience. As soon as you can, reflect on what went on in the call. Do you think it went "well" or "badly"? What do "well" and "badly" mean to you? Do you remember feeling a moment of awkwardness after saying something? That may be because you slipped back into some subtle form of pushing or exerting pressure. Did you sense any withdrawal or pulling back? Debriefing is a useful way to keep track of how your new Unlock The Game habits are developing.

- **Stop thinking "sales script" and retrain yourself to think "conversation" and "dialogue."** I talk every day with people who say that their scripts make them feel uncomfortable, even robotic. Scripts may give you a feeling that you're in control, but that's an illusion. I know that thinking about "conversation" and "dialogue" can be scary—it means you're admitting giving up some illusion of control. But you're dealing with another human being—how does trying to control them build trust?

I promise you selling can be a positive and productive experience if you are open to shifting to a new mindset.

About the Author:

Ari Galper *is the creator of* Unlock The Game® —*a new sales mindset that overturns the notion of selling as we know it today. He is also the founder of* Unlock The Internet Game® *that takes his new sales mindset and applies it online to build trust with website visitors. You can take a FREE TEST DRIVE of Ari's approach here at* www.UnlockTheGame.com, *or if you have an online business visit* www.UnlockTheInternetGame.com

CHAPTER 6

5 Success DNA™ Principles ALL Entrepreneurs Need to Know!

Maria Gamb

What makes some people successful and some not so successful? Passion? Drive? Focus? Yes, those are all important attributes, but what comes before that? What is the foundation for success?

In starting my business, I realized there were some very important issues I needed to deal with in order to make it happen. Most burgeoning entrepreneurs start off with their concept, financing and marketing strategies etc. But after successfully surviving 20 years in corporate America, an unsuccessful business venture, and now experiencing a successful, lucrative entrepreneurial business, I've learned that there is a definite DNA to being successful. It's the stuff that's deep down—how we're wired inside that actually attracts success. That means not only the financial rewards and more time to enjoy life with family and friends but the quality of those relationships.

I discovered that the following 5 principles make up our Success DNA™. They are the essence of the belief systems that will bring you what you want in your business and in your life. They serve as a solid foundation to build upon.

Each principle is wrapped around the powerful boomerang of the Law of Attraction. By making some conscious decisions about how you perceive and think about success, you realign the principles of your Success DNA™. The dynamic of the Law of Attraction is very simple:
If you Think It
You Attract It
And then you Manifest It

Change your mindset! Dump the outdated limiting beliefs and get ready to succeed! Once we get out of our own way—anything is possible!

1. DEFINE THE CHARACTER OF SUCCESS

Close your eyes and think about the most successful person you know. It doesn't matter if they are someone you know personally or someone in the public eye. It actually doesn't even matter if this is someone you admire or not. Now I am going to ask you three questions about this person:
How did they get to be successful?
What kind of character do they have?
How do they live their life?

Based on those answers you will have a pretty clear idea of how you perceive success. This is the template for success that is imprinted in your mind, and it is the information that the Law of Attraction takes action in your life. I can hear you drawing an exasperated breath. Ah yes, my friend, it's true. Warp perceptions of success yield warped realities of success. If you believe that successful people are selfish, uncaring and manipulative—well that's pretty much what you would manifest unconsciously for yourself.

So, how about taking a different point of view?

If you had the opportunity to create the "Success Superhero" what would that powerful person be like? How would they behave? What kind of character do they have? Since I'm a visual person, I always start with the outfit. They need a cape, some snazzy tights and fabulous accessories (definitely an awesome purse!). A modern day Wonder Woman of sorts! She would be compassionate, giving, respectful, patient, and generous with a fantastic sense of humor. Integrity and honesty are an important part of how she deals with her personal and professional relationships. She enjoys collaborating with others etc. I think you get the point.

Now define the character of your Superhero. Be very specific and detailed about the kind of successful person they are, including what their personal relationships and life balance is like. It is critical that you are clear about this because this is an essential foundation principle.

2. Redefine Your Relationship with Money

So many women feel that dealing with money is too hard, too time consuming or overwhelming. Some were taught that only men handled money. Others were taught scarcity and lack, or at times have not felt deserving enough to have extreme wealth.

There is a tug of war relationship that goes on which creates a very stagnant dynamic around money and the acceptance of abundance for many people. They are literally short circuiting the flow of money into their lives with their thoughts.

Remember that the Law of Attraction first starts with what's going on inside your head. If deep down you truly don't believe that you will be able to create a truly abundant business let alone make enough money to just get by, yet you're using daily affirmation about money, you'll find yourself struggling to tread water. Simple physics is the easiest way to explain this situation.

A Positive (the affirmations) + A Negative (fear around money) = A Neutral

That means nothing happens. You've just cancelled out your Universal flow of money and abundance in your life. So let's go back to our "Success Superhero." She consciously makes the decision to recreate her beliefs around money, refusing to let old patterns govern her future. After all, she's got some new killer boots to buy to go with that cape!

3. Choose Ease!

Get rid of the old tapes that say, "You need to work doubly hard if you want to be successful as an entrepreneur". Refuse to listen to people who tell you that you'll need to give up all your time and energy to be a success. Run from folks who sit around saying "this is hard."

You have a choice. You can accept these old limiting beliefs that you need to sacrifice yourself for success or you can choose to enjoy the process and find the entire experience a pleasurable adventure filled with ease. How you experience your process is all about your perception of how one achieves success. Go back up to the first principle: how does your superhero achieve success? Struggling? Living in fear of paying the next bill or locating the next client? Or does she surround herself with a terrific coach to help her create the business of her dreams? Perhaps she has a supportive virtual assistant who can help her handle some of her workload. Is she part of a mastermind group where she can learn from other entrepreneurs how to work more effectively and efficiently? All these components help to create ease.

4. Allowing

Are you allowing yourself to be successful? Sounds like an outrageous question doesn't it?

If the doubt that you can achieve success or have abundance is still intact, then you cannot "allow" your desires to be manifest. I think Michael J. Losier explains it best in his book "*Law of Attraction*" with this summation; "*the speed at which the Law of Attraction responds to your desire is in direct proportion to how much you allow.*" It's as simple as that. Remove the doubt around the desire and you'll begin to manifest what you really want quicker.

5. Gratitude

Be grateful for all that you have no matter how much or little you perceive that you have. No matter what challenges you may face along your journey to creating your business or the relationships in your life, never forget to express gratitude. The Universe appreciates a grateful person and will return to you other grateful people in your life.

After all my years working in corporations and with entrepreneurs, I can tell you that people who are grateful are more productive, happier and healthier. They also laugh more than other people I know. Gratitude is a sign of humility, generosity and celebration. Share this type of celebration with others. In doing so, you impart to them the gift of example and inspiration.

Learning how to make the adjustments to these Success DNA™ principles in your life will serve as the foundation for you to build your business upon.

Oh, and by the way, that Superhero we've been talking about is actually you! The DNA you decide upon will serve as a beacon in the Universe activating the Law of Attraction to bring you more of what you want.

Just remember—the Universe will happily oblige you. If you think you need to struggle to succeed then you will. Personally, I am choosing to have lots of fun building my business. Delicious happiness; Amazing Clients; Supportive Mentors; Abundant Finances; Endless Opportunities, and the ability to travel the globe to satisfy my "inner gypsy."

What are you choosing for yourself?

About the Author:

Maria Gamb, *"The Anti-Sabotage Expert" from* NoMoreSabotage.com, *coaches female entrepreneurs and other highly motivated professionals to overcome self-sabotaging limiting beliefs about money, relationships and success, allowing them to manifest abundant and successful lives without boundaries. Join the FREE* No More Sabotage! *ezine TODAY and receive the FREE BONUS GIFT* 89 Ways Women Sabotage Their Financial Success. *Visit* www.nomoresabotage.com

CHAPTER 7

How to Overcome the Paralysis of Entrepreneurialism

KATHY HAGENBUCH

As I anxiously sat staring at my endless list of great moneymaking ideas and partially completed projects, I frantically wondered how many of the most urgent I could possibly focus on at one time and actually complete.

I was once again reminded of something profound that I had run across in the endless maze of information out there…'If you can do it all yourself, your dream isn't big enough'!

Acutely aware that there was nothing wrong with my dreams, I reflected with tremendous frustration at all the times I had hired 'qualified' people to help me only to be left with critical pieces hanging in the balance. Projects that when finally completed, were way past deadlines and not even close to the quality I had expected and paid for. Furthermore, I was positive that if I just could find more hours in the day, I could certainly have done these things much better myself with much less stress!

Were my expectations too high? Was I really demanding too much and being too judgmental? Why did others not have the drive, commitment and discipline that I have to follow through? Was there something wrong with me? How could I fix 'me' when I wasn't convinced that there was something wrong with me in the first place?

Somehow these questions sounded vaguely familiar. Suddenly thoughts of conversations with my solopreneur and small business clients came hurtling back to me at the speed of light.

And then it hit me! I was suffering from the very same maladies that I helped countless business clients work through themselves! An obstacle I called 'Entrepreneurialism' was paralyzing me.

As I answered some of the questions myself from my Entrepreneurialism Quiz, I was painfully aware that I was indeed suffering from entrepreneurialism. Does any of this sound familiar to you too?

- Yes—I was burning the candle at each end and couldn't seem to catch up
- Yes—I felt that no one could do things as well as I could
- Yes—It was clear to me that if I wanted things done right I would need to do them myself
- Yes —I was judgmental and frustrated when others didn't live up to my expectations
- Yes—I found it difficult, if not impossible, to delegate tasks to others
- Yes—I knew I had everything I needed to be super successful but for some reason never quite seemed to be able to achieve the level of success I knew I was capable of
- Yes—I had many great ideas and not enough time to implement them
- Yes—I felt scattered, unfocused and completely overwhelmed
- Yes—I had a sense of urgency that someone else was going to think of my great ideas and implement them first

I realized that if I were to ever have a chance at overcoming this entrepreneurialism block and creating the business and life I wanted, I would need to embrace the very core concepts of the Six Figure

Success Program that I encourage my clients to consider for themselves.

I reflected on how each of the core concepts of business mastery are all interconnected and applying each was critically important in my quest for a successful business: a business that I enjoyed and didn't run me, and a lifestyle that allowed me the leisure, freedom, flexibility and security to fully enjoy myself and my family.

I was at that pivotal moment that many entrepreneurs and small business owners face – I had to make some changes for my business to thrive and flourish or stay stagnant where I was.

While each of the Six Figure Success concepts is absolutely essential for that growth, at this very moment, those that I needed to focus on most to move my business to the next level became crystal clear for me.

First, since I am an idea generating machine, (but also an absolute master at making things as complicated as possible); I had to focus on simplicity and completion, not perfection. Plus I would need to systematize and automate everything I could, without removing the human element critically necessary for creating successful business and personal relationships.

Second, since there was no way for me to do everything myself, I had to enlist the help of others. The most successful people I know understand that they do not know everything and can't do everything themselves. These successful people seek to fill the gaps in their knowledge or ability with people who excel in areas they do not.

They realize that having a success team is essential to reducing feelings of being overwhelmed, becoming more efficient, effective and productive, and for getting the necessary support during the journey. Your success team will be the key to allowing you to take full advantage of the 20% activities that produces 80% of your results.

Although this has been a difficult area for me to focus on, it has also been the most significant – both in terms of allowing me to tap into my own brilliance and to zero in on the exact 20% activities that produce 80% of my results, revenue and success.

Converting Your Success Team into a Lifetime of Revenue

As I looked at the checklist from my Six Figure Success Team Builder Program, I re-focused on filling each of the eight categories of my success team with people whose expertise complimented and exceeded my own.

Nagging doubt continued to creep up the back of my neck. How would I cultivate the relationships with my success team to create win/wins for everyone involved and convert them into a lifetime of referrals and revenue? What would make this team any different from all the unsuccessful attempts I had made in the past?

The difference this time is that I now knew how I was 'wired'. I would actually need to implement the knowledge I had discovered from scientifically validated assessment results that show the way we are 'hardwired', drives our behaviors and our actions. It also dictates how we communicate with others and how we 'show up in the world.'

When we understand our own behavioral design then we can better understand and appreciate the behavioral design of others.

The way we each walk, talk, think, react, solve problems, make decisions, use time, the degree to which we take risks and say what's on your mind, whether you focus on people or results, are all the result of how we are naturally wired.

All these observable human behaviors which sometimes appear to be less than perfect (and often even rub people the wrong way), are the very traits that make it hard for me to delegate effectively to others and accept excuses. These are the traits that demand the best from me and others, drive my sharp tongue and lead to great frustration when people don't do things as quickly or as well as I would like.

Once I understood this about myself, I could actually see those same things in the people I surrounded myself with or encountered and worked with on a daily basis.

We all handle problems, challenges and decisions in our own way. We all deal with people and influence others to our opinion differently.

We all move at our own pace, uniquely respond to change and to the pace of our environment, and each of us reacts differently to rules and procedures set by others.

Understanding how people do these things lifted a weight from my shoulders and allowed me to view the world from a totally different perspective.

I now *get* how important it is to make changes in the way I show up in relationships in order to empower others to feel good about themselves.

I decided I would no longer look at the behaviors and traits of others as weaknesses, negative or broken and needing to be fixed. I understand that each of us is wired differently – none of which is right or wrong, just different.

And in each and every human encounter, it is my choice to consciously adapt my style to honor the styles of others. While at times making those changes can take patience and great restraint, I now have the freedom and flexibility to do so with greater understanding and minimal cost and energy to myself.

As a result of this extraordinary knowledge and choice, I've had to let go of some of my judgments about people and how they do things, but it has truly been the most significant moment in my business. Without this freedom, I would have continued to be frustrated and my business would eventually have become boring and stagnant.

I now enjoy each and every moment and look forward to finding ways to create win/win relationships that not only help me to accomplish more but also to help others succeed with their dreams.

Be Bold, Outrageous and Have fun!

"People rarely succeed unless they have fun in what they are doing."
—Dale Carnegie

Finally, almost as important as everything else I've talked about, is this simple yet profound thought that I would like to leave you with.

While our future and the future of our families is serious business, taking things too seriously will only stifle our creativity and ability to accomplish things effortlessly and elegantly.

While each of the areas I have discussed is paramount to your success, the most important of all in overcoming 'entrepreneurialism' and in creating your successful business and dream life is to be bold, daring, outrageous and have fun! Enjoy your journey as much as your destination.

About the Author:

Kathy Hagenbuch *is the creator of the* Six Figure Success Series Programs *for entrepreneurs and small business owners, including the* Success Team Builder Program, Six Figure Systems *and* Six Figure Communication. *Discover the exact income producing activities and low to no cost marketing strategies that will allow you to immediately find MORE TIME, make MORE MONEY, while WORKING LESS and having MORE FUN. Visit* www.SixFigureSuccessSecrets.com *for Kathy's free e-course* Insider Secrets to Creating Six Figures and Beyond.

CHAPTER 8

3 Simple Secrets to Manifest a Six (or Seven) Figure Business

CHRISTINE KLOSER

Do you want to manifest a six or seven-figure business? If you're like most business owners the answer is a resounding "yes"! In fact, it's the most common reason clients hire me. They're ready for the "next big thing" that will help them make a difference, make lots of money, and enjoy life.

You may be thinking it's impossible to make tons of money and live the quality of life you deserve. I'm here to show you that it's possible. How do I know? Because I made it possible for myself.

I wish I could tell you it was an easy and a joyful journey at every turn, but that wasn't my situation at all. You see, I discovered what I'm teaching here by attending the "school of hard knocks." Just a few years ago, I remember lying on my bed in my tiny apartment in Venice, Calif. in tears. My husband and I had just decided it was time to call a bankruptcy attorney.

We owned a yoga studio in an elite neighborhood in Los Angeles that had failed. Our expenses exceeded our income by nearly $7,000 per month. We tried keeping the business afloat by draining our personal savings and maxing out our credit cards, only to realize there was

54

no way out. So, there I was, with tears in my eyes, my heart beating out of my chest, hands shaking… as I called the attorney.

After hanging up the phone, I sat for a few minutes taking some much needed deep breaths, when I became aware of a feeling inside of me. I felt a nudge to call the attorney back to tell him I wouldn't be filing for bankruptcy. In that moment of silence (and deep breathing), I realized I had everything I needed to rise about my circumstances and discover a way to create a new life amidst the reality of my horrible financial situation.

At first, even I thought I was crazy, but after discussing it with my husband, we decided together that we'd make a new choice to create a new reality for ourselves. So we did.

What follows are the three most critical secrets I discovered on my journey from the verge of bankruptcy to a multiple-six-figure business. But first, I need to caution you. These are three simple secrets, not three easy secrets. Just because something is simple, doesn't mean it's easy. You may even notice that the opposite is true; it's the simple things that are the most challenging to grasp.

As you read through the rest of this chapter, it's a good idea to keep a blank piece of paper next to you. Use it to jot down the thoughts, ideas, hunches and action items that enter your mind while you're reading.

Secret #1: Aligned Intention

"Work joyfully and peacefully, knowing that right thoughts and right efforts inevitably bring about right results."
—James Allen

Aligned intention is where your success begins. Aligned intention occurs when what you intend to accomplish/manifest is deeply aligned with your heart, your soul, your purpose and your Divine calling in life. As an entrepreneur, your business is an expression of who you are in the world. It is as much a personal development experience as it is a business development experience.

Think about a time in your business when everything happened

Power and Soul

effortlessly; when you literally felt like the planets were aligned just for you. You were in the flow, your intention was absolutely aligned and you felt great.

Now, think of another time when you felt like you were pushing a boulder uphill. You set out to accomplish something, but it drained your energy; it took more effort than you thought; nothing was working and you were stressed-out and frustrated. It's safe to say your intention was not aligned.

How do you know (before you set out on a plan) if your intention is aligned? It's simple, but not easy. It requires you to turn off the noise in your mind, your computer, your negative voice and be still. Yes, I'm talking about slowing down to the speed of silence. In silence, with closed eyes and deep breaths, ask yourself if what you intend to do feels right. Then stop and notice the feelings and thoughts you experience. You may feel your body (or even hear a voice) saying "yes" or "no", or maybe "not now." You may be given critical information that guides you toward an aligned intention.

Until every cell in your being resonates with a "yes," continue going back to the stillness and ask for guidance that ensures you are doing the right thing.

Secret #2: Purposeful Planning

"If you really want something, you can figure out how to make it happen."

—Cher

Once it's clear your intention is aligned and you are setting out in the right direction, it's time to create your Purposeful Plan. This is where most creative entrepreneurs fall short. I speak from my own experience when I tell you planning is an essential part of success. It's true you can "wing it" and experience success, but only to a point.

This was a lesson I learned the hard way. I had unintentionally turned a hobby into a business several years ago. Since the business happened without my intention or a plan, it ended up controlling me. I spent six years and invested tens of thousands of dollars trying to catch up to it, but never did. My hobby was running on a wing and a prayer... and I was funding it! It took me two years of feeling like the business was heading south until I actually looked at the numbers. Once I faced the reality of the numbers, it became clear the business had run its' course.

I sometimes fantasize about what "could have been", if I had a plan in place. It's not easy to think of the multi-million dollar opportunities that passed me by because I was "winging it." So, when I tell you a Purposeful Plan is essential, I mean it whole heartedly.

Don't worry, you need not buy fancy software or hire a professional to write a fifty-page business plan. Your Purposeful Plan is not for the bank, it's for you and your team. And, it's simple but not easy. I recommend working with a coach or trusted friend and simply begin having a conversation about your vision, mission and objectives for your business. Record your conversation, then go back and listen to it to pull out the words, phrases and sentences that resonate with you.

Next, with your vision, mission and objectives in mind, identify four to six strategies you'd need to implement to achieve those objections. Then, set forth creating a plan including the specific "to do's" and due dates. Congratulations! You've just completed your plan!

Secret #3: Accountable Action

"Have a bias toward action—let's see something happen now. You can break that big plan into small steps and take the first step right away."

—Indira Gandhi

With your plan in place, it's time for the "rubber to hit the road", and Accountable Action is where it happens. One of the issues entrepreneurs face is a never ending "to do" list. Often times, your highest priority items get pushed to the bottom of the list because you're busy with everything else. Here are two ways to make your actions accountable so you guarantee they get accomplished.

Accountability to People: There are two ways to be accountable to people. You can hire a coach who will ensure you focus on your highest priorities (and purposeful) tasks. Or, you can work with an accountability buddy (a friend, colleague, spouse) to keep you on track. Just be sure to set up an accountability structure with your buddy that works for you. I recommend at least a once a week check-in, and have many clients who choose to do a daily check-in. This is a sure-fire way to fast track your success.

Accountability to Dollars. You may be asking yourself what this is. Let me explain with a story. When my daughter was born, I decided to step away from my business for one year. Then, when I was ready to return I needed something to kick me into high-gear fast. I invested nearly $15,000 in a high-level Mastermind program (with Alexandria Brown) because I knew if I put that much money on the line I would not let myself off the hook. I'd be accountable to getting a great return on my investment. This approach is not for everyone, but if it is right for you, it's the single fastest way to put your Aligned Intentions and Purposeful Plan to work.

As you step further on your journey to a six (and seven) figure business, these three secrets will guide you at every twist and turn. Wherever the journey takes you, you'll never get lost when you use these secrets to combine the power of intention, the value of a plan and the energy of action.

About the Author

Christine Kloser, *an internationally recognized business coach and consultant, is the Founder of* NEW Entrepreneurs, Inc., *the* Conscious Business Circle, *and President of* Love Your Life Publishing. *She's a former television host and has appeared in numerous radio and television programs and has been featured in Entrepreneur Magazine, the Los Angeles Times, and Woman's Day. Get her FREE special report* How to Avoid the 3 Massive Mistakes Made by Most "Conscious Business" Owners *at* www.ConsciousBizReport.com

CHAPTER 9

Casting a Smaller Net to Receive a Higher Yield!

P.K. ODLE

When I started my Feng Shui consulting business in 1997, like many new business owners I was certain that everyone would benefit from my services. Plus, I had a burning desire to make a difference in the world by improving the lives of my clients through Feng Shui. I knew all buildings have a combination of sabotaging and supportive influences on the occupant's health, relationships and finances. I wanted to show my clients how to enhance the supportive energies of their homes and businesses and neutralize the sabotaging ones, thereby creating a better life for themselves and their families.

At that time, I thought my biggest problem was how to reach potential clients, because just like a doctor, my hands are tied until my services are requested. I attempted to connect with potential clients by:

- Attending networking meetings several times a week
- Giving lectures to any group that expressed interest
- Being interviewed by the media
- Buying all sorts of print advertising, including a series of advertisement articles.

Thanks to the popularity of do-it-yourself books, many people had heard of Feng Shui. Most thought Feng Shui was a religion, a super-stition, or an intuitive art like a psychic reading for a building. I began teaching at the world renowned *American Feng Shui Institute* in 1998, which made it easier for me to focus on educating people that Feng Shui is actually a sister science to Acupuncture, and that they share a 5,000 year history of improving people's lives. As with any science, whether it's Feng Shui, Acupuncture or Western medicine, there are no 'one-size-fits-all' solutions or remedies.

I wrote articles to explain that a comprehensive on-site Feng Shui analysis of a building includes complex calculations based on the specific 15° compass orientation of the building and when it was constructed. These calculations reveal each building's unique energy blueprint. Plus, the dates of birth and gender of the occupants must be factored in, because each individual has a unique relationship to the Earth's magnetic field. I wanted my readers to understand that barely 5% of Feng Shui consultants worldwide can determine all of their 'Feng Shui Personal Directions,' including their Prosperous, Consuming, Analytical, Creative, Valued Friends, Lonely Pillow, Rob-bery, Injury, Fragile Luck and Romance 15° directions.

Without a marketing background, it took me awhile to realize that when it comes to marketing and advertising, trial and error is time consuming, ineffective and expensive. I can see why most small businesses close their doors within the first 5 years. However, thanks to referrals and persistence, my consulting business was still going well by 2002. I spent every waking minute marketing my services, plus a ridiculous amount of money on print advertising that was more edu-cational than promotional. Fortunately, that's when I met Christine Kloser and joined her networking group, *N.E.W. Entrepreneurs*, where I began learning more effective marketing and advertising methods from their guest speakers.

The first thing I learned through *N.E.W.* was the importance of highlighting the benefits of every feature. Why should someone care about their 'Personal Directions?' Because they can hold on to more of their money, like Christine and her husband did once they stopped using their main entranceway. That door lay in Christine's 'Consuming Direction.'

Some energy combinations are cyclical and occur annually or in 20 year periods, such as a 'Money Lock' that prevents money from coming to you. If you know your building's unique energy blueprint, you can avoid a 'Money Lock.' I saw this in action with the shoe company *L.A. Gear.* Prior to studying Feng Shui, I was the on-site travel agent at *L.A. Gear* when they consolidated from three buildings in Marina del Rey, California, to one building in Santa Monica, California. For three years I watched the thriving shoe company dwindle away to nothing. Out of curiosity, I did a Feng Shui analysis of the building and discovered that it was in a 20 year 'Money Lock.' A few years later, I met a man who worked for a company that moved into space that *L.A. Gear* had vacated. He told me his company had gone out of business too, and I surprised him by saying that it must have happened before 2004 when the 'Money Lock' was released. I was right.

One of the most important marketing rules I've learned is that it's crucial to keep in touch with potential clients on a regular basis. When Alexandria Brown, the *'Ezine Queen'* spoke at *N.E.W.*, she made me painfully aware that unless I kept in contact with potential clients, when they were ready to make an appointment they could just as easily hire the next Feng Shui consultant that crossed their path. In September 2003, thanks to Ali's tutorial, I launched my own email newsletter, *The Feng Shui Advantage Monthly*, and in less than a year I had 1,000 subscribers. I wish I had known how valuable a newsletter was when I started my business, mainly because of all the thousands of people who met me once, yet may never benefit from my services because we have lost touch.

As many of the guest speakers at *N.E.W.* became my clients, they all encouraged me to focus my advertising on a specific target client, especially Alexandria Brown, Kim Castle of *BrandU* and Lorrie Morgan-Ferrero of *Red-Hot-Copy*. I resisted their advice for several years for a couple of reasons. First, I suffered from a slight case of insanity. You know… when you keep doing the same thing over and over again expecting different results. I thought if I just kept at it, I would eventually reach more people with a general message of how they could benefit from managing the existing Feng Shui influences on their lives. But I finally decided they were right.

It was a real struggle to decide on exactly which type of client I wanted to target. At first I considered targeting families because in Classical Feng Shui health and relationships come first. After all, money can't buy good health and harmonious relationships. Plus, I thought of the client whose four children with Attention Deficit Disorder started doing their homework sitting with their backs toward their individual 'Analytical Directions' and how all their grades improved.

By 2004, I'd taught over 1,500 on-site clients how to identify and manage all their 'Personal Directions.' That's when it struck me to create a 'Personal Directions' report and make it available separately from an on-site consultation. Thanks to the vision of Kim Castle of *BrandU*, I expanded my original idea (a personalized report based on an individual's gender and date of birth), into the *'Lifetime Keys Personal Directions Self-Mastery Toolbox.'* It's the only complete toolbox with all the supplies and step-by-step guidance necessary for anyone to manage all their 'Feng Shui Personal Directions' anywhere in the world. I could see this product helping children and adults for their entire lifetime.

Later, I began to think about all my self-employed clients who had doubled and even tripled their income after following my Feng Shui advice. Working from home actually makes the Feng Shui of your house twice as important. Lorrie Morgan-Ferrero of *Red-Hot-Copy* said she reached an annual income of over $100,000.00 for the first time when she moved her back toward her personal 'Creative Direction' as she worked her magic writing copy that really sells. Even Lorrie and Kim's skeptical business partners now sing the praises of Feng Shui because both of their companies continue to expand each year.

I finally realized that home-based and solo-preneur clients are my favorites when a client I hadn't seen in years stopped to visit with me after a lecture I'd given at a Home Remodeling and Decorating Show. I was elated to hear that her business had tripled, her husband had received a promotion with a substantial increase in salary, and that both their sons were acting in commercials, television and feature films without having an agent. She said her husband had always been skeptical about Feng Shui, but now he's the one who makes sure to order their Annual Update each year to keep all their remedies current. After that wonderful encounter, I knew exactly the type of clients I wanted to attract: ones like her.

Once I was able to define my ideal client, it became easier to write about how they would benefit from following my Feng Shui advice. After many years of struggling to reach everyone, I'm finding it far easier to write advertising copy, articles and my newsletter when I visualize I'm writing to one specific person.

Now I agree with the experts that identifying your best client is like money in the bank. By casting a smaller marketing net, I'm receiving a higher yield for my efforts. I've by no means limited myself to only working with solo-preneurs just because I'm directing my ad copy toward them. Like a good doctor, I'll always remain available to assist anyone who wishes to follow my Feng Shui advice and reap the benefits.

About the Author:

P.K. Odle, *founder of* The Feng Shui Advantage, *is a widely recognized Classical Feng Shui consultant, instructor, speaker, author and publisher. Her specialty is working with solo-preneurs from chiropractors to info-preneurs, restaurateurs to retailers, artists to attorneys, from start-ups to expanding businesses. Visit P.K.'s website at* www.FengShuiAdvantage.com *to receive her free Special Report* 5 Secret Obstacles to Your Prosperity… Revealed! *and her award winning ezine,* The Feng Shui Advantage Monthly.

CHAPTER 10

From Mangos to Mansions

Frederic Patenaude

I've always been interested in earning a living doing what I love. I never wanted to work for a big company, or do the 9 to 5, every day, seek "security" and get stuck in the rat race. I wanted to be master of my own destiny, and do what I love, always.

I was 20 and I had an education in music. My native tongue was French, my English was good but not fluent, I had no particular competency, and I didn't really know how to use a computer... but I had a passion. I was seriously interested in alternative nutrition and health, specifically the philosophies of "natural hygiene" and the "raw food diet."

In 1997, I left my hometown near Montreal, Canada, for the sunny city of San Diego, California. Without much of a plan, I took a bus to California, and ended up working with a young company who were selling books in my subject of interest.

My career started with an apple. For several years, I was the editor of a health and raw food newsletter called, *Just Eat An Apple*. It was there that I developed the writing skills, exposure and reputation within the health community that allowed me to create my own websites.

The Internet was growing a lot in those years, but I had yet to learn how I could actually make money on the Internet. At first, I just wanted a website to share my passion. I wasn't thinking in terms of profits.

My dream became to be able to work from *anywhere*, with only a laptop, and make a living doing what I love. I knew that I had to get on the Internet to make that happen. I had been online since 1998, but it took me a long time to understand how to make money with it.

At the time I didn't have much going in the way of products and I wasn't sure where it would go, but I knew I was excited about the possibility of making a living using the world wide web.

One day I got the first piece of advice that helped me build my dream. I learned that the sole purpose of my website was to build a mailing list. My friend and mentor at the time, Olivier, told me, "Fred, your website has to sell your readers to the idea of signing up for your list... and from there you turn them into customers!"

So slowly but surely, I built that list... to about 5000 people.

I was sending out a monthly newsletter with recipes and health information and made sure it was unique and personal. But I still couldn't find ways to truly make it profitable.

My niche was fairly limited. I was writing about one of the most radical diets: the raw food diet., There are thousands of people in the world who are interested in learning more about this way of life, and since information online was limited and with my own interest in it, I was able to build a list of enthusiastic readers.

I authored some books that were on sale on my website but I was far from understanding the power of the information products.

One day, my friend Olivier, who had learned a lot about Internet Marketing but didn't have a website of his own, decided to test his knowledge on me. He challenged me to try his methods. Olivier had been telling me for years about the power of information products, but I still didn't really understand the concept. Once I did, everything changed.

The method I followed is as follows:

1. I asked my list of readers what their biggest problem was about trying to eat a healthy diet.
2. We identified that the main problems were cravings and bingeing
3. We wrote a sales letter about a product that would solve that problem.
4. In less than a week, we created that information product (a digital manual and some audio files).
5. We sent an e-mail to my readers list announcing the product was available.
6. We watched orders flow in ... almost magically!

This magic happened when I started to understand that I simply had to build my lists, ask them what they wanted, give it to them and I could make a great living doing what I loved!

Now, with over 32,000 subscribers and several websites, I am thrilled to be not only making a living online, but living the life of my dreams by sharing a message of health and personal empowerment with tens of thousands of people all over the world.

The online lifestyle has allowed me freedom and power. I have been able to travel to Brazil, Costa Rica, Bali, Tahiti and French Polynesia, Spain, Italy, Germany and other places, always with my laptop, of course! At first, I had to manage the business from abroad, but now the business manages itself.

I see a lot of people trying to achieve the same but without great results. Many try to become "overnight successes." They work at it... sporadically, get involved in the latest "offer of the week," try all the web optimization software out there and give up after a few months.

One day I learned from a very successful business coach that you can "take five years to become an overnight success." The truth is we often see the results yet fail to recognize all the hard work and time that was invested to make it happen.

It took me years to get to where I am and I'm sure I could do it now in a fraction of the time. But above all, it's about your message and your passion. The more passion you can develop for what you do, the more likely you will be to become successful.

Passion is something that can be cultivated and can fluctuate, and you have no idea sometimes what kind of work you'll be passionate to do or what kind of niche will interest you.

When I was in high school, we had some "career orientation" courses that I didn't take very seriously. I was smart enough to understand that I could design my own career.

What's ironic is the kind of work that I'm doing today wasn't even possible when I took these courses. The world has changed so much since then that one could not have predicted that this way of life — working at home making a living on the Internet—would be possible. At the same time, we have no idea what the online future holds.

I have come to realize that my online mailing list has been my biggest 'treasure box'. I open it all the time to find hidden gems.

I have found most of my staff on my mailing list. Just one e-mail to the list was enough to find people almost begging to work for us.

I have been able to travel the world to several countries for free—just from contacts I made from my mailing list.

I have had opportunities, made beautiful friendships, and found the woman of my life, Tera, who first worked with me as my assistant and then became my life partner.

Everything is possible with a mailing list. Things can happen at light speed and cash can be created on demand.

I have learned as much from my readers as they have learned from me. It's not just about selling 'stuff'. It's about developing relationships with a group of readers and clients with common interests.

Recently, our online business and mailing list brought to us a tremendous opportunity and we have decided to invest in a rustic retreat center in the beautiful country of Costa Rica.

Our offices are currently located in a gorgeous beach town on the Pacific Coast of Costa Rica. We have a beautiful retreat center where we invite clients for private seminars and quiet retreats. We're surrounded by protected national parks, beaches, waterfalls and tropical rainforests.

Watching the sunset over the ocean while checking how the online sales are doing on the laptop is now a reality. And it became real because that's what I saw as my dream many years ago.

My work now is about sharing with others the tools that I apply to get the life and the health I want. With over 10 years of passionate study and investigation into the raw-food and natural diets, I have designed specific health programs to take people to the next step in their health evolution.

We also host powerful seminars in self expression, making a living doing what you love, and more.

About the Author:

Frederic Patenaude, *originally from Quebec, Canada has been helping people improve their lives in many different ways since 1998. Through nutrition, fitness, and self-improvement strategies, his clients experience boundless energy and the rewards of success. His website has over 300 pages on self-improvement and how to create the best diet and health program without gimmicks or nonsense. To sign up for one of his free mailing lists visit* www.FredericPatenaude.com *and* www.SmilingMango.com

CHAPTER 11

Never, Never, Never Quit!

JEANNA POOL

On my desk, I have a paperweight with a quote from Winston Churchill that says, "Never, never, never quit." I also have an old Chinese proverb taped to my computer monitor that I read every single day. It says, "The temptation to quit will be greatest just before you're about to succeed."

So, why I am I telling you this?

Well, we have to go back in time a bit, to when I was a little girl. You see I am the only child of two very successful entrepreneurial parents. In fact, my mother is one of the hardest working, most successful entrepreneurs I know. This year she is celebrating her 40th year in business and she taught me one very valuable lesson, which is: "Never, ever quit!"

This lesson has helped me time and time and time again in owning my own small business. And it will help you too! Whether you are just starting your own small business or have been in business for decades, you will get discouraged. You will want to quit. You will want to throw up your hands and shout "Enough! I've had it! I am going back to a 'real' job." I guarantee this will happen to you. It's not an if, but a when.

You will want to quit.

Don't. Don't you dare quit! Bite, scratch, claw and do whatever necessary to make it as a small business owner. The benefits far outweigh the negatives. They really do. If they didn't, one in every three Americans would not venture out on their own as new small business owners.

Don't quit seems pretty easy to commit to, doesn't it? Well, I can predict and tell you right here and now what will happen in your small business—I guarantee it.

You will do everything right. You will market yourself consistently and repeatedly. You will read every book and attend every seminar and do everything in marketing you know you are supposed to do. You will network until you can't stand-up any more. You will develop the most effective, kick-butt commercial for your small business possible. You will spend money to market yourself. You will market, market, market…

But, at some point after doing all of this, at some point of doing everything right), you will want to quit. Business will slow down or come to a complete standstill. This whole "marketing thing" will seem to not be working.

But, again I'm telling you: never, never, never quit. Period.

Let me give you a real life example from my own life. Awhile back I had one heck of a three day stretch in one very long week.

I woke up Monday morning and thought to myself, "What's the point? Why am I doing this? I am a successful graphic designer, web designer and marketing consultant. I market my business exactly the way I teach my clients to market their small businesses. I market my business consistently, over and over and over again. Even when I am jammed with business, I am still out there marketing. But, what's the point?" I continued to ask myself.

You see, that Monday was just one more Monday in a long string of what seemed like forever 'Monday's with no new clients. I had gone about six weeks without signing one single new client, which for my business is very, very rare and a definite dry spell.

I was marketing myself consistently. Every single week I was actively marketing. I promise you, I absolutely practice what I preach, teach and do for my own clients. But still, nothing. Zilch.

I started to get that low-grade almost panicked feeling of the internal voice saying, "Hello, Jeanna, you have bills to pay. You have a mortgage. You need clients in order to eat. Hello, why isn't your marketing thing working?"

Tuesday morning was even worse.

The panic thoughts in my head were going crazy. Just about then I made the "mistake" of going to the mailbox to check my mail." Oh, great! Four big bills to pay. Yippee! I am so glad that I have no new clients."

But, then Wednesday completely turned the week around. It's almost as if God whacked me upside the head and said, "Duh, Jeanna. Never, never, never quit."

Wednesday morning is my weekly referral group meeting. When the time came to pass referrals, I received two—one for a brochure project and one for a direct mail campaign. These referrals were done deals—new clients ready to do business. It was simply a matter of signing the contracts and getting started

Then, on the way back to my office, I checked my voicemail. One voicemail said, "Hi, Jeanna, this is ___. I was referred to you by ___. I have looked at your website and I am ready to hire you to design a website for my small business. I'd like to meet this week to get started." The second voicemail said, "Hi, Jeanna, this is ___. I was at the workshop you gave last week. I heard every word you said and I want to hire you for marketing help. Call me so we can set up a time to get started."

Holy cow! Four new clients in a matter of hours! But, it gets even better. After I got back to my office and finalized everything with the two blazing hot referrals and set up appointments for the two new clients that hired me via voicemail, I got one more call. It was from a prospect that I'd spoken with over a year ago. He called and said, "Okay, Jeanna, I have taken enough time on the fence. I know I need help. I am ready to hire you for the marketing project we talked about last May."

I hung up the phone and had to sit down to keep from falling down. Five clients in less than three hours! Proof and a reminder to never, never, never quit!

Here I was doing everything right, but not seeing the *immediate* results from my efforts. I was ready to quit. But, I didn't quit. I never, never, never, ever quit, because my temptation to quit was greatest right before I succeeded—five clients in less than three hours.

And, my friend, this will, at some point, happen to you. It's life. We're human. In fact, you may have already experienced it. You will do everything right. And you will hit a dry spell. And you'll want to quit.

But again, I tell you, never, never, never quit.

Beginning and running a small business is hard work but, it is so worth it and you will make it. You will succeed. But, you have to remember and commit to what my mom teaches: never, never, never quit!

If you quit, how will you know if you quit right before the flood gates opened up for you? How will you know if you quit just before your best client in the history of your small business were about to hire you? How will you know? Fact is, you won't. So don't quit. Ever!

Oh, one more thing. That day, that same Wednesday that I got five clients in less than three hours, as I was packing up to leave my office for the day, my phone rang again. It was another prospect, who said, "Hey, Jeanna, this is _____ from _____. Remember me? Well, I'm finally ready. I want to hire you to help market the new business venture I have been talking about. What does your schedule look like the rest of this week?"

Make that six new clients in one business day...

I wish much success to you!

About the Author:

Jeanna Pool *of* CATALYST creative, inc., *is an award-winning graphic designer, website designer and marketing expert. Jeanna works exclusively with small business owners who are struggling with marketing themselves and attracting clients consistently.*

Jeanna is the author of When Your Small Business is YOU™ Marketing Handbook. *Visit Jeanna's website:* www.MarketingThatWorks.com *and download your FREE copy of her special report* 5 BIG Marketing Mistakes That Can Bankrupt Your Small Business and How to Avoid Them Forever.

CHAPTER 12

Are You on Board Your Own Train? 5 Key Steps to Visibility, Credibility and Profitability Now

Joy Schechter, The Event Trainer™

It was almost Thanksgiving and I hadn't decided where I was going to spend this day. I could take a plane and fly 3000 miles to visit my parents; *or* I could drive 30 minutes to see my friends; *or* I could take a 3 hour train ride to visit my cousins.

All great places to enjoy Thanksgiving... but what would be the *best* choice? Which would give me the highest gain? What would I miss out on? Which would give me the least hassle? Who would I disappoint the least if I didn't spend time with them? What would it cost me to go?

All of these are the same questions I used to ask myself when deciding which clients or projects to take on. At best, I was cutting my losses, and at the least, merely getting by day-to-day. This was *not* why I went into business for myself. I love what I do. I love producing successful and *profitable* seminars and workshops that help business owners enhance their business visibility, credibility and profitability. I used to think that by putting the client's needs first would insure I'd have clients—or so I thought.

It was more like the tail waging the dog.

It never entered my mind to say, "What would *I* like to do to simply just enjoy my day?" Once I sat down and started to look at what *I* wanted, my business started to turn around and—wouldn't you know it—I started to enjoy myself. The pressure was off. There were some customers who just disappeared once I realized I had a direction different from theirs. It was clear we weren't on the same path and it became a simple solution to connect them to someone who was. A win for both of us.

But I'm getting ahead of myself—there's much more to be learned on my Thanksgiving journey….

So, I had a choice to make—where would I go?

STEP #1: PICK A DESTINATION.

I decided to take the train to from Los Angeles to San Diego. I love trains. I love the journey, the vista, the adventure of not knowing whom I'm going to meet along the way—it's my vehicle of choice. I know I'm headed toward San Diego, but *how* I got there was all up to me. I could have taken my car and driven down and back whenever I chose, listened to my CDs, sing to myself... but that's all about me, all by myself. I could have taken a bus and let someone else do the driving… But I'm truly limited to someone else's pit stops. I don't get much room to move about and it's cramped, confining and…

STEP #2: BUY THE TICKET. SHOW THE UNIVERSE YOU ARE COMMITTED.

I chose to take the train so I could ride in comfort, ease and freedom to move around—truly a vehicle all about my comfort and ease. That's how I wanted my business to go: with comfort and ease. My business flows when I choose the right vehicle to reach *my* destination. I stopped trying to sell anything and everything to get hired by clients, and focused on *how* to make the events I ran a profitable extension of their business, in alignment with my client's vision. Have you ever noticed that in your business too?

Step #3: Get on board: take action!

It takes energy and effort to climb up the stairs onto the train. But what if it's really all about traveling *your* tracks to success? Destination doesn't show up as a reality until you take an action. Action + Action = Momentum. Momentum gets your train out of the station and on its way to your destination.

Step #4: Invest in your own train.

You won't get the ride if you don't get on board. I emphasize *you on board*.

Have you ever tried to get a customer to buy into a service or product when *you* weren't truly committed to? Ouch. Let me tell you, that hurts and I've been there. Wandering about… no direction… hoping to make it… down the road… someday… no ticket in hand. *Not even on board my own train!* I came to realize that even though I had a great train with a great ride, until I got on board—I couldn't get *my train* out of the station. You have to believe 100% that if you're not riding your own train, who else will be? And you *want* to be on board your train.

Step #5: Enjoy *the ride*.

There's nothing like *the ride*. You look out the window at all the vistas, and you see parts of the scenery and buildings (normally hidden if you drive a car and too small from a plane). There are aromas on the train ride, from sumptuous leather seats, delicious foods and the different stops en route when the doors open outside to trigger your imagination. There are club cars and sleeper cars, first class and coach, baggage cars (feel free to leave your "baggage" behind in that car—you can always pick it up later!). There are so many ways to experience this journey. Best of all are the people who come and go. You may never know their names but you will have the most wonderful conversations with opportunities to assist people or discover someone who'll assist you.

You have to get on board your own train, heading to your own destination, in a manner that reflects you. Enjoying the ride happens when all the elements of the ride are in alignment. I think it's the ride that brings out the best in people on trains.

Does any of this sound familiar? Setting up your business based on what others want? *Living someone else's ride?*

As I worked with my clients to bring their destination to reality, what I discovered was that if my clients didn't follow the "train steps", not only was their event NOT a success, but it literally derailed their business. The business and the event must move in the same direction or *the train becomes derailed!* You are the Engineer of your (event) train. When you take ownership and get on board your *own* train, others will *want* to pay you to ride, and people will get on board your train to buy your products. Visible. Credible. Profitable. This only occurs when you authentically can get on board *your own train* and most of all, enjoy the ride yourself.

I found that once my clients got their business aligned with their goals, they found clarity and experienced a world of freedom to play, create and invent. It became a chain reaction where their clients experienced that freedom as well, and it kept filtering down and down. I found that in my business also. I hope you'll find it too.

Here's what I've learned from riding on trains:

Step 1: Pick a Destination

You can't lay down track until you know where you are going. Make a decision, any decision, and head in that direction. If nothing else, you'll be in motion. What, where, when, how.

Step 2: Buy a Ticket

If you don't have a ticket you can't get on board. A ticket lets the universe know you are committed. You are now in alignment with your destination. The train won't start up until you commit.

STEP 3: GET ON BOARD

The train will never leave the station until you get on board. There's work to be done and it starts with *an action*. Take a step. Climb on board. Take *your* seat and prepare for the journey and adventure to begin.

STEP 4: INVEST IN YOUR OWN TRAIN!

Think about the journey you've been on, where you've been and where you are going. Most rides are pretty great and are powerful to share. Get on board and invest in your own train. You are the Engineer of your business, taking your clients to new destinations. Your team is bringing up the rear in the Caboose. Consider this—What kind of ride you will be giving your passengers? What kind of service will they get? What products can they buy on the way that will support their travels?

STEP 5: ENJOY THE RIDE

Every train ride has great vistas along the way. The passengers who get on and off the train are people who will cross your path. Some will bring new light to your ventures, some will cause chaos—test your will to keep traveling—and some will become great travel partners for new adventures, reaching destinations only previously imagined.

About the Author:

Joy Schechter, The Event Trainer™, *brings over 15 years experience in the event, seminar, and hospitality industries in producing successful and profitable programs. From content design, onsite management through product sales, her work with businesses masterfully uses Seminars and Workshops to increase their profits from mere hundreds, to hundreds of thousands of dollars, as well as through her ongoing teleclass series. To find out more about consulting, classes, or e-newsletter contact:* joy@TheEventTrainer. com *or 310-308-6444.*

PART II

Turning Your Dreams Into Reality

CHAPTER 13

Manifesting a Dream From Within a Nightmare: Strategic Living and the Five Key Milestones to Manifestation

Christine N. Cibula, M.S. & Katherine Cibula

Have you ever had a hard time making your dream become reality? Well, we are in the business of manifesting dreams! For fifteen years I have been dedicated to helping businesses take an idea from concept to completion. I personally work with top-level executives within companies, listen to what they want to accomplish, and create a dynamic system to make it happen. I have consistently heard one comment from these individuals as their projects reach completion, "You made my dream come true." Nothing is more rewarding.

MANIFESTING A DREAM FROM WITHIN A NIGHTMARE

How often have you heard that great ideas come out of moments of desperation?

Several years ago, I had a major health crisis. Time was of the essence in getting the treatment I needed to expect a full recovery. Speed was essential. The learning curve was steep and the information overwhelming. I needed the information in a distilled manner. It was not available. When I encountered one hurdle after the other, I needed help to find my solution. Help was not available. In the business world, they say, "Find a need and fill it." I began to see the transferability of what I was experiencing personally into the business world.

It was clear that I needed to stay financially viable. I had to act fast and modify my existing consulting business that required working in the office and face-to-face meetings into an Internet consulting and service-based business that enabled me to perform the same responsibilities primarily from my home office. I also needed to do it fast. During that time, my mother and I became business partners and we laid the groundwork for Strategic Living, Inc. using the exact techniques I describe below.

OUR GREATEST POWER COMES FROM WITHIN

Dr. Edith Eva Eger, a world-renowned Clinical Psychologist and Auschwitz survivor, is both a mentor and colleague. She is an expert on thriving, not merely surviving, after experiencing tremendous adversity. She addresses thousands in her keynote speeches and advises, "Write out the words 'I AM POWERFUL' and place it on your mirror. Each day, look into your own eyes in the mirror and repeat the affirmation, 'I AM POWERFUL.'"

Dr. Irwin Katz, President of International University of Professional Studies (IUPS), uses a therapeutic process to remove old patterns of thought and replace them with new patterns of thought over time. He calls this effective process "clearing the vessel".

I personally experienced that our greatest power is the power of choice in our thoughts. For in deciding what we want let go of, keep, and manifest, we have already embarked upon an amazing journey. If we can see it in our minds, feel it in our hearts, and desire it in the core of our beings, then we can hold it in our hands, and we can live into the reality we are creating for ourselves.

Defy Defeat!

Most businesses (85%) quietly close their doors within the first year, and of the remaining businesses (15%) only half survive the next five years. Clients need the process of information distillation because they are already overwhelmed with too much information. They often don't know how to effectively integrate the information into their business model. More importantly, they need problem-solving resources that can do it for them. Speed saves time and money. It can be the difference between success and failure.

Five Key Milestones to Manifesting A Dream

There are five key milestones to manifesting a dream that we consistently stress with our clients in the process of taking the client's dream and making it a reality.

Milestone 1: It All Begins With a Thought

At Milestone I, we encourage clients to gain clarity about what they want to achieve. Some call it being in thought. Some call it meditation. Some call it creative visualization. Some describe it as listening to an internal voice.

We provide the client with exercises that allow them to imagine the experience they want to live into. We then work with clients to clarify their thoughts. We do detailed intake interviews and provide challenging questions to gain insight, clarity, and focus. We call this process "distillation of thought".

In our business, my mother and I share the better part of our time focusing on outcomes and visions we have for our business. We literally "dream together" on road trips up and down the coast of California, driving across country and during late night conversations on the phone. This process is called "masterminding" wherein a third "master mind" emerges that is a shared collective consciousness.

Milestone II: Thought Into Action

At Milestone II, clients know what they want to achieve, but they have no idea how to get from point A to Z. We work with clients to help them to gain clarity. We break down each thought into actionable steps and funnel clients toward the resources they need to get the results that they want. If clients do this process on their own, it can take months to find the information, resources, and experts, which we provide instantly. We shave years off of the learning curve to assure the highest probability of success in the least amount of time.

We also go through the steps with clients to bring their thoughts into the present. We write down what clients think and feel. It can be a simple positive lead-in statement, such as, "I am grateful now that I am…" or "We are…" or "The business is…" and then plan the process of living into in the present tense. We utilize exercises where the client imagines it with all of the senses. See it! Taste it! Hear it! Smell it! Feel it! Touch it! We make it real in the present.

Milestone III: Mapping the Plan

At Milestone III, we work with clients to map a cohesive results-oriented business plan. We believe that a one-page visual representation is extremely useful in order to "see" the plan to stay focused each day.

Mapping the plan is a key element in the creation process. You do not need to know how you are going to make something happen. Rather you need to see with clarity what you are in the process of creating. Clarity and focus increase success. Map into place everything you know. Be specific. Vision the outcome in your mind and put as many details as you can into what your ultimate vision will look and feel like.

Milestone IV: Implement

At Milestone IV, we work with clients to take what they have developed throughout the previous steps and put it to work for them through implementation. This is often a place where clients face a lot of hurdles, mainly because they have no idea how to access the information they need to implement effectively. Hence, they start "spinning their wheels" in their head rather than being effective by doing a little each day. We help clients to efficiently structure their time for maximum gain.

When the opportunities present themselves, we encourage clients to take action in the moment as long as it fits or improves upon their business model. Otherwise, these activities become unnecessary distractions. Persistence is a primary characteristic of successful clients. They keep going come rain or shine. They consistently fine-tune their knowledge base and believe in the power of their dreams. They are fully vested and keep going until they succeed. Bob Proctor refers to this as 'praxis'—the integration of belief with behavior.

Milestone V: Marketing Through Press Releases

At Milestone V, we launch a 6-month to 1-year search engine optimized press release campaign to maximize the visibility of the client's business via the Internet, the primary research tool used by businesses. In the movie "Field of Dreams" the famous whisper is, "If you build it [the business] they [the clients] will come." While clients may start coming, the reality is that they may not start coming in droves. The business may falter due to a lack of proper marketing. Once you have built it, time is of the essence in making it successful. I've worked with many clients who have said, "HELP! I've built it. They haven't come! What now?"

Don't panic when you face this business situation, because we can help you. Our press releases get 5 times the visibility of a standard press release. We are experts at search engine optimizing your business exposure so that clients find you time and time again. We do more than simply create a press release. We build sustainable attention and interest into your PR campaign to achieve long-term visibility.

Be Brilliant

Marianne Williamson shares, "We ask ourselves, 'Who am I to be brilliant, gorgeous, talented, fabulous?' Actually, who are you *not* to be?" Each of us has the power within us to manifest our dreams. When power is linked with the soul and the dream, it is an unstoppable combination. Let your light shine. As Thoreau so beautifully inspires, "Go confidently in the direction of your dreams! Live the life you've imagined."

About the Author:

STRATEGIC LIVING, INC. is a Public Relations and Business Consulting Firm. **Christine Cibula, M.S.** *is President and CEO,* **Katherine Cibula** *is Vice President. Focused on empowerment of the small business owner, services include targeted search engine optimized press releases, specialized project management, and business development consulting. If you're inspired to manifest your dreams by driving traffic to your products and services, register NOW for your FREE HOW-TO E-COURSE AND EZINE at* www.Strategic-Living.com. *Get started today!*

CHAPTER 14

Blast Through Obstacles: 5 Ways to Zap Through Barriers to Achieve Your Dreams

Joan Clout-Kruse

"How do you handle the obstacles that get in the way of achieving your goals?"

That was one question I asked many Silicon Valley business people that I interviewed a few years ago. They do not experience those stomach-churning feelings of fear when building their businesses. They do not get stuck when it doesn't work out the way they expect it to. They just move ahead and find another way to accomplish their goals because they are having fun doing what they do.

Discover below five ways that dynamos think, and how they zap the obstacles, catastrophes, and barriers from their lives to successfully achieve their dreams.

1. Unmet Challenges

The day I asked my obstacle question to Cesar Plata, the networking guru of www.InfoBayArea.com, he seemed puzzled. He paused for a moment, looked at me, and then questioned me with one word, "Obstacles?" I nodded yes and remained silent waiting for his answer.

"As with anyone launching a startup business," the trail blazing entrepreneur said, "I have endured many personal and financial sacrifices and struggles. I did not see these efforts as barriers; I accepted them as learning experiences. The way I see it, they were simply unmet challenges."

"Unmet challenges?" I asked curiously wanting to know more.

"Yes," he said. "When something doesn't work right, you try another way, and another until you achieve the results you want. In my mind there are only unmet challenges."

"Oh, I get it," I thought. You just keep on going until you reach your goal. You stay focused and keep on trying until you succeed.

Unmet challenges: Cesar opened up a whole new world for me on how to handle my goals. Forget obstacles. Stomp out the word, roadblock. Break away from fear. Block out stuck. Don't say, "I can't do it." Instead I must say, "That step didn't work, I'll try the next one."

Each time I work on my goals now, I relax, take a deep breath and just do it. Every step of the way along life's journey I know that I will handle those unmet challenges with ease.

2. Expect Success

"I expect to succeed," said Jinsoo Terry in answer to my question. Jinsoo, a multicultural expert in San Francisco, continued, "When a business executive says 'no' to me, in my mind I am already saying 'next?' I am thinking of the next person I will ask."

Jinsoo puts on motivational shows that have original rap and hip-hop music. She finds the best people in their business to help her create a phenomenal entertainment and motivational program. She writes the music, creates the video for the show, and invests lots of money to develop and produce an amazing extravaganza to inspire and entertain her audience.

Jinsoo called me recently and said excitedly, "Joan, you won't believe this!" (Well, I have learned that I will believe it when Jinsoo tells me.) "I got a call from one of the biggest banks in Korea. They want me to do a television show for them next month."

Jinsoo's advanced preparation paid off. She was already halfway finished with the show she was creating and will use it for the upcoming television show. She believes that if you prepare something with a future job in mind, the opportunity will come.

When rejection comes your way, just say "next!" Be prepared like Jinsoo. Tell your friends about your passion, and the opportunity will come.

3. Be Persistent

"I believe that it is better to try and fail than to never do anything at all," said Nancy Kruse, a director on the animated television series *The Simpsons*. "Whatever we want is ours for the asking," she continued.

In 1989 Nancy heard that a new animated television series was planned for production. No successful adult animated television show had come out since *The Flintstones*. She yearned to be a part of this new show. She showed her student film and sketchbook to the producer of *The Simpsons* show. She told Nancy that "someday" she'd be a great animator. Nancy thought "someday" meant not now.

Yet she was persistent. For the next two weeks Nancy called the producer everyday. Finally, her persistence paid off and she was hired as a background artist. She had no idea what that was but she trusted that she could figure it out. She did and she is doing what she loves.

Today, *The Simpsons* holds the Guinness Book of World Records titles for "Longest-running Primetime Animated Series" and has been bestowed with 21 Emmy Awards. Nancy never let an obstacle get in her way. To learn and grow along the way we just have to believe that we can do it and be persistent.

4. Ask For Help

"Just do it and ask for help," said Gail Turner in answer to my question. She was the first woman to build, and fly solo, an experimental airplane across country.

It all started in 1975 because some pilot friends jokingly told Gail,

"A Kindergarten teacher can't build an airplane." That was exactly the motivation Gail needed to commit herself to doing it. She wanted to do something unique that no woman had done before, even though she knew nothing about building airplanes and was very new at flying them.

She built her first airplane in the living room of her Belmont, California home in 1975—airplane parts strewn in every room of the house. Her girlfriends helped her drill holes, glue fabric, and iron the fabric to take out the wrinkles. In July 1977 the "Fly Baby" and Gail were off to the Oshkosh, Wisconsin, the "air shows of air shows," sponsored by the Experimental Aircraft Association. She made history by being the first woman to build and fly solo an experimental airplane across country.

Gail built a second plane with the help of many friends. She learned the true value of surrounding herself with talented people. Her friends supported her new dream and helped her build the plane. "Although I didn't know it at the time, I was way over my head when building the second plane," she said, realizing what a great team she had.

With persistence and tenacity you can make your wishes a reality. Get a good team together to help you achieve your dreams and the team will solve any obstacle that comes along.

5. Have Fun and Go For It.

"Follow your bliss," said Doug Jones, CEO of Mortgage Magic in Silicon Valley. "When you do that you can turn over any obstacle that gets in your way. You just keep on going until you meet your goal."

Doug Jones was raised in the Great Dismal Swamp, at the corner of North Carolina and Virginia. His family was so poor that he rarely wore shoes, and at the age of ten he was sent to an orphanage where they measured his IQ at 95. He graduated at the bottom 25 percent of his high school class. Most people would think that Doug, with his upbringing, would struggle emotionally and financially his whole life.

Doug broke that stereotypical mold. For 20 years he worked in finance and then one day at church the minister gave a sermon entitled,

"Follow Your Bliss." He was so inspired that he quit his finance job the next day, and on April Fool's Day in 1990 he created Mortgage Magic with $600.

One day Doug sent me an e–mail message that read, "Have a great day. I am so happy. I just want to pass it on." That was all he wrote. Enjoying life, having fun and giving to others are part of Doug Jones's philosophy for a content, healthy and successful life. "Life is meant to be fun and to be enjoyed," he said. Doug's entrepreneurial spirit inspires and impacts his employees who are all encouraged to have fun and give back to the community.

Recently Doug told me, "When you have a clear vision about your dream, there are many, many people who get excited and will help you achieve the dream. The way to overcome an obstacle is to share your vision and passion then allow and accept help from others."

I don't know about you, but every time I read these stories I tell myself that I have no excuse. I can do anything that my mind can create. I can jump over barriers to get where I want to go. No obstacle is so strong that I can't break it. All I have to do is believe in myself.

Isn't it great to know that we have the power to succeed? We can dream and begin our journey to success. It happens every day to people like Jinsoo, Doug, Nancy, Gail and Cesar who believe that they can do it. It can happen to you, so start dreaming today, believe in yourself, build your team, and take action. Remember…obstacles are just unmet challenges. Have fun and follow your bliss.

About the Author:

Are you ready to put your company on the map, get recognized as an EXPERT, and attract new clients? Let "The Entrepreneurs' Book Coach," **Joan Clout-Kruse** *help you create a book to get the recognition you deserve. Author of the popular book,* Top 10 Traits of Silicon Valley Dynamos, *and the e-Book,* How to Write Your Great Book in 90 Days. *Get Coach Joan's FREE AUDIO and guide on "Are You Ready?" at* www.powerhousewriting.com/are-you-ready.html

CHAPTER 15

Achieving The Dream (or Learning to Let Go)—Faster Than A Speeding Bullet! One Woman's Journey Out of the Corporate World

Lisa U. Crisalle

The Daily Grind:

I'll never forget that day! It was a Friday night. I'd just come home from my usual 80 hour workweeks. I was exhausted and drained from the demands of managing a 20 attorney law firm. My boyfriend Lucho (who is now my husband) and I sank into the couch, both of us in a daze. We sat there, looking into each other's eyes.

"How can we keep doing this? We never get to see each other. We're working until we are beat, and we have no energy to spend quality time together," I said.

Each of us normally left the house at 6:00 a.m. and returned home between 8:00 and 9:00 p.m. every night. Lucho owned and operated his own company. I kept the books and managed his accounting over the weekends, while handling the demands of managing a major law firm during the week.

Something had to give.

We both agreed that once Lucho's company made a certain dollar amount, that it would be an appropriate time for me to quit the law firm. I wanted to work with him full-time. At the time he was consulting for another company while running his own business, and I was concerned that if I left the law firm we would lose my additional $97,000.00 yearly income.

Lucho looked into my eyes and said, "Lisa, it is time for you to quit your job."

I inhaled deeply, stopped breathing, and felt my eyes open wide. I felt terrified. "Lucho, I'm scared to let this go."

To understand who I am, I need to tell you that I have been living on my own since I was 17 years old. I had always supported myself, sometimes working as many as three jobs, while going to college to complete my degree.

After moving from Oregon to California, I got a job with a prestigious law firm. Little did I realize, as some adventure novels begin, that I would spend the next 20 years in this high-stress corporate environment.

Starting as a receptionist, I learned and moved on as a legal secretary. Later, I obtained my certification and specialized as a Litigation Paralegal, then utilizing my education and moving on to Marketing Director, and ultimately to Law Firm Administrator. I also maintained and continued my connection in the fitness industry as an instructor and trainer for everything from swimming, skiing and martial arts, to aerobics, and indoor cycling. To put it mildly, I was busy.

I built a career in law. I excelled at juggling many roles and responsibilities, everything from human resources, law firm marketing, information technology (computer systems), accounting (budgets, forecasts, investments, etc.), contract negotiations, mediating disputes, crisis management, book editing, event planning, space planning, and chief cook and bottle washer! I loved the challenges, the responsibilities and the personal growth and education learned throughout the years. I made myself indispensable to the law firm.

Yes, there were days that I would completely "lose it." When I didn't think I could be stretched any further, the other part of me knew that not only could I handle it, but the law partners relied on me to "handle it." I was a sharp and respected problem solver.

I worked hard to be recognized in the community as a professional career woman. In Orange County, I was active on several boards, organized and marketed several large events in our legal community. Yes, I hobnobbed with Judges, Senators, and Congressmen and women. And, I was well dressed, wore wonderful suits and fabulous high heels!

The fear of letting go, of walking away from this known "life", scared the hell out of me. How could I, would I, turn and leave everything that I'd worked for? I'd built up security, established an admirable professional identity, and wonderful, important relationships and personal connections.

How would I take that "leap of faith" and trust in the universe that things would work out for me?

BREAKING THE STATE:

This is when Lucho worked his magic on me. As a Master Practitioner of Hemispheric Integration (HI) and Neuro Linguistic Programming (NLP), he taught me how to access the information available in both of my brain's hemispheres providing me with new options. I could begin to see the resources needed to resolve inner conflict I never knew existed.

Lucho was teaching me, through these processes, the secret to supercharging my vision for truly fast results. Now, here were clear and specific strategies to create a road map for my future with tangible results to keep me motivated. I could see the way to success. Utilizing whole brain thinking, I was learning to stop "driving from the trunk" and take charge of my life.

Using these amazing tools, Lucho guided me in doing a self-inventory of how I truly felt. He asked me "when you say that you feel scared, what image comes to mind?" I thought for a second and responded.

He asked, "As you think of that image, what is your internal dialog? What do the voices in your head say to you?" Lucho guided me in becoming aware of my heart rate and my breathing. He then asked if I felt tense or relaxed. He had me memorize that experience. Then he did something called "breaking my state" and asked me to spell my name backwards.

I later found out that spelling my name backwards allowed me to clear my mind so that the next image would not be influenced by the first one. I was allowing myself to experience what was coming next, from a fresh clean slate.

Lucho then asked me to think of a time that I felt truly excited. And, as I recalled that time, he quietly asked me the same questions about my breathing, my heart rate, relaxation or tension.

As I did this, a smile spread across my face. I was a step ahead of him, as I compared what I thought was fear, to what I knew, was excitement.

There was no difference. Could it be, that I was really *excited* about changing my life, and not scared in the least bit?

"Now, Lisa, I want you to compare the two." We both started laughing as we realized that I already had.

I was speechless, and even more excited as I realized that my job did not define who I was, but that I defined what and who I wanted to be. Lucho reminded me that choice is better than no choice. Now I had the ability to choose the life I wanted.

The life I chose was to walk away from the corporate world. And I never looked back.

Of course, I had some adjusting to do. I had to get used to not being interrupted every 3 ½ minutes with some emergency or issue. In fact, I initially had some "activity" withdrawals. And now, there isn't enough money or large enough salary, to drag me back.

ACHIEVING THE DREAM:

Here I am today, four years later, celebrating my one-year wedding anniversary with Lucho. I am sitting on the balcony at the St. Regis

Hotel, overlooking the Pacific Ocean and the beautiful swimming pool. Reflecting on this past four years, I understand the meaning and the value of the lessons and why I am here, in this beautiful location, with my most remarkable husband, living this amazing life.

As I sit here on the balcony, I look up and see a spectacular golden hawk fly overhead. And, instead of it flying by, it seems to hang out above me, sending me a message.

According to ancient Native American teachings, the hawk is seen as having keen eyesight, it is about opening our eyes and seeing that which is there to guide us.

The hawk's message is about Strength, Foresight, and Truth. I interpret it as a message of Love, Freedom and Perseverance. It represents the Strength, Foresight and Truth of who I am, and how far I have come. I look up, grateful.

About the Author:

Lisa U. Crisalle *now works directly with her husband (nutrition expert, Lucho Crisalle, RD), bringing their company* Exercise & Nutrition Works Inc. (ENW), *to the forefront of the nutrition and health community. They currently work with Gold's Gym International and Max Muscle Incorporated. To learn more about Lisa, Lucho and ENW, and receive your FREE Special Report:* "The Truth About Fat Loss and the Way to a Leaner You – Revealed!" *visit* www.ExerciseAndNutritionWorks.com *or contact Lisa at* Lisa@ExerciseAndNutritionWorks.com

CHAPTER 16

From Welfare to Millionaire

SANDY FORSTER

I gaze out my large windows at the swimming pool, see lush palm trees swaying in the breeze and watch the sun sparkling on the surface of the beautiful Mooloolah River as it gently flows to the sea. I live in on an island (I LOVE being able to say that!), in a beautiful executive home with a waterfall; drive a stylish silver Landrover Freelander; travel overseas whenever I fancy, attending all the personal development workshops and seminars I want. I take myself and my children on wonderful adventures around the world and have a lifestyle many people adore. I'm a Success Mentor to tens of thousand of people, an international speaker, a bestselling author and internet marketing guru!

As I write this, I feel a sense of gratitude flood my body as I gaze upon the luxury yachts and multi-million dollar homes surrounding mine and reflect on my journey over the past 4 years from welfare to millionaire.

After my husband left me with a 6 month old and 3 year old I lived in constant struggle for many years. I was working seven days a week in my clothing business which I no longer enjoyed, had over $100,000 of debt and was surviving financially through welfare. My future looked bleak and to say I was stressed about money was an understatement.

My entire life revolved around money or, more precisely, the lack of it. Money consumed me; frustrated me, annoyed me and scared me, and it most definitely eluded me. When it came to creating wealth, I felt powerless, hopeless, useless and worthless. I knew deep down inside I was a good person, so why was my life such a shambles? What had I done to deserve this? "What was wrong with me?!"

Then I discovered there's a secret to getting everything you could ever want in life. There is a law, a Universal Law, which states, "We attract whatever we choose to give our attention to—whether wanted or unwanted." The result of this law is, if you continue to focus on the lack and limitation in your life, you will continue to create and attract more lack and limitation. If you instead focus on the wealth, abundance and prosperity that is already present in your life—no matter how small it may currently be—then you will instead begin to create and attract more wealth, abundance and prosperity.

For some people, this comes naturally. For others (like me), this can be a slow and arduous journey. Through my many money failures, mistakes and unwise decisions when it came to practical money-making steps, I have been fortunate enough to develop a passion for 'what makes people rich'. It is through this passion that I have been able to create my own incredible wealth, and now, share these secrets with people across the globe.

My first thought was "Okay, just focus on prosperity, wealth and riches, then that's what I'll attract." However when you're raising 2 small children on your own, have $100,000 of debt, making $15,000 a year and constantly can't pay the bills, keeping your focus on abundance is NOT an easy thing.

However, you have a choice as to where your energy or attention is focused. You can choose to focus on what is working in your life and what you want more of, or you can choose to focus on what isn't working and what you don't want. Either way you get more of whatever it is you focus on.

I adore sharing everything I know with anyone who will listen—including my children, constantly telling them, "What you focus on becomes your reality." When I was in my stage of attracting money but it was flowing out just as fast, my daughter would say, "blah blah blah. We don't need a lecture about that spiritual stuff, it doesn't work anyway—we've still got no money."

And that was the truth. We were still struggling financially even though I was saying my affirmations and visualizing what I desired a couple of times a day. The problem was, the rest of time I was seeing bills and feeling my solar plexus tighten. I was experiencing fear, worry and panic about where the money would come from, that I would never have enough, that I would be struggling forever.

I had to stop and look at what I was creating for myself when my daughter was around twelve and came to me the day before her school dance and said, "Mum, I need some new shorts for the dance."

Now I need you to really get this picture—I was having a really tragic week financially. I'd had a check bounce, a few bills had come in, including a red-letter bill (those scary ones), and I was beginning to go into my usual panic mode around money.

So the conversation went a little like this…"Can you buy me my shorts and shoes, I really need them?" "Darling, I don't have the money right now." "You never buy me anything; I have to have them!" "Darling, I said I don't have the money." "Can't you just put it on your credit card?"

The credit card was up to the limit, so that wasn't an option and by this time I'm starting to freak out. I am seething with all sorts of very negative, very strong emotions. Frustration, because even though I was making good money, it was disappearing; embarrassment, because I felt so hopeless at managing my money; guilt, because I felt like a bad mother for not being able to buy things for her; sadness, because I knew how disappointed she would be because she'd be missing out once again and anger, because she was asking me for something I just didn't have. Unfortunately, anger was winning, and the picture was not pretty.

The veins on my temples were throbbing, my eyes were bulging out of their sockets, I was hissing through gritted teeth, had spit flying out of my mouth and I'm sure there were traces of steam coming out of my ears as I screamed like a banshee going to war "I don't have the money to pay all our bills! I've got to try and pay the phone bill before they cut it off. We just don't have the money—don't you understand? We're broke right now! WE DON'T HAVE ANY MONEY!"

She looked me squarely in the eye and in all the wisdom of her twelve years upon this earth said to me in her most disgusted tone, "Well, if that's how you FEEL whenever you think about money—the Universe is NEVER going to make us rich."

In that moment, plain as day, I could see why I was still struggling financially. I was attaching my strongest emotions—all negative—to the one thing I wanted most. And in doing so, I was repelling it. I was pushing money away. I was making sure it didn't stay long enough for me to enjoy.

My emotional outburst was not about having money; it was about NOT having money. So 'not having money' was the dominant vibration or energy (or order), that I was sending out to the Universe day after day. And the Universe was picking up that 'not having money' order and giving it straight back to me, day after day.

I was blessed to be shown that although I thought I was focusing on the prosperity I desired, I was actually focusing on what I didn't want, and so kept re-creating it over and over. Since that fateful day, by changing my focus and cultivating a 'Millionaire Mindset' I have gone on an amazing journey from marketing a personal development course to becoming a Life Coach, to creating a number of highly successful coaching and mentoring businesses which focus on showing others how to create a life filled with prosperity, abundance, success and happiness.

I have gone from welfare to millionaire through doing what I LOVE. Now I teach others how to take their hobby, interest or passion and turn it into a business so they too can spend each day doing what makes their heart sing. I show people world wide how to tap into that limitless stream of prosperity, abundance and success through the metaphysical AND by applying simple practical strategies.

What was my biggest challenge—relentless money struggle—turned into my biggest opportunity—teaching you how to be wealthy, abundant and RICH beyond your wildest dreams! I offer free resources at www.WildlyWealthy.com and show others across the planet how to be Wildly Wealthy FAST though live seminars and workshops and generally get to spend my days 'playing' at what I love. Life doesn't get much better that that.

The best thing is, I share my knowledge with conviction—knowing that although I had no great education, no money behind me, no connections and no real idea what I was doing, simply by persistently and consistently visualizing, affirming and focusing on what I DID want, I have been able to create a life I love.

Remember, no matter what life throws at you don't give up, keep focusing on what you DO want—because if I can do it, anyone can—including YOU!

About the Author:

Sandy Forster *is an International speaker, Millionaire Mindset Mentor, Bestselling Author, Award-Winning Business Owner and mother of two beautiful children. Sandy has a passion for showing others how to create a life filled with richness, prosperity, success and happiness in an easy to understand, empowering and extremely fun way! Visit her websites today for your own FREE prosperity resources - www.WildlyWealthy.com and* www.SecretMastermind.com

CHAPTER 17

Soul Power: How I Went From Soul-Destroying Job, to Scraping-By Entrepreneur, to Creating a Life of Joy, Passion and Purpose

BONNIE HUTCHINSON

MOMENT OF TRUTH

I turned into the alley behind my office building to park in my spot. A truck was blocking the alley. I burst into tears.

"What is happening to me?" I asked my passenger. "I've raised two kids on my own, gone back to school as an adult, done amazing things in my community—and a truck in the alley wipes me out?"

My first entrepreneurial venture did not begin as a dream. It was an escape from a nightmare. However scared I was of starting a business, I was even more scared of what would happen to me if I stayed in my "safe" government job.

SEARCH FOR ESCAPE

I thought my next career move might be to start a business. Maybe a book store—I love books. In the meantime, I knew I had to leave my job or die. I tried to get another job—one I didn't hate—that paid enough to cover expenses while I learned to start a business, but every job I pursued bombed out.

One day there it was: A community organization wanted to contract someone to organize family education programs. The position was half time, for one year. When I saw the ad, I got shivers.

Maybe I could start a business selling my expertise in how to make things happen in a community.

This contract would cover the mortgage. Maybe in the other half of my time, I could get contracts to cover groceries. In a year I would surely find other projects.

As I was on my way to an interview for the contract, my son said, "Mom, are you sure you know what you're doing? This is your son the poor starving university student speaking."

I laughed and said, "No, I'm not at all sure," and went out the door and into life as a solo entrepreneur.

Without knowing it at the time, I was using soul power. I now know to trust those shivers that are followed by a whole new way of looking at something.

I've never regretted my choice to go it alone, but I have had stressful times and times of huge learning. Here are some things I've learned so far.

EXPECTATIONS = INCOME

Everyone I talked to said I needed enough savings to live for six months to a year, until the new business could support me. That was good advice. I often wished I'd taken it.

In fact, I was barely solvent. After years of shoe-string salaries in the non-profit sector, raising kids, and going to school, I still often lurched from paycheck to paycheck, juggling bills and credit card debt. I had enough savings to last maybe two weeks—or one really good day!

The first year I appreciated doing work I enjoyed for people I liked. It was wonderful not to dread work every day. I was grateful to make enough money to scrape by.

Then I noticed other solo consultants seemed to earn more money than I did. I found out a man whose work I thought was much inferior to mine got paid several times more than I did.

After I muttered about a sexist world, a wild new thought occurred to me. Maybe customers thought he was worth more because he asked for more. I took a deep breath and raised my rates. People paid. I took another deep breath and raised my rates again. People paid. I came to believe that I could earn a comfortable income. And I did.

My next transition was bigger. If I could move from scraping by to a comfortable income, perhaps I could take it further. Maybe I could earn a six-figure income. I began to think of wonderful things I could do with a six-figure income. I imagined myself in that situation. Lucrative projects showed up. A six-figure income was easy to attract.

Again without knowing it, I was using soul power. I now know that the universe mirrors back to me what I truly believe and intend. When I splash around in the energy of what I desire, it shows up in my life.

Perfect customers

From the beginning, I only worked on projects I considered worthwhile and ethical. Within that boundary, I pretty much said "yes" to any project that people asked me to do. I was afraid to say "no" for fear no other projects would show up.

Over the years, I had a few "projects from hell" with unpleasant clients. No amount of money was enough to compensate for the misery. Worse, while I worked on those projects, they sucked all my energy and there was no space for happier projects.

As I became more confident about raising my rates, I also got more selective about my clients.

I now only work with people I like, whose values and goals I respect, whose projects I enjoy, and who believe I am worth every dollar. Interestingly, as I let go of what's less-than-perfect, I attract more perfect customers.

My soul power lesson is this: be clear what you want to attract, and be prepared to let go of some things to make space for what you do want.

A spiritual gift

As I grew my business, I became increasingly passionate about spiritual growth. The underlying theme of my personal life was to understand more of my spiritual self—my soul.

I learned more about tuning into intention and integrity. I learned to discern and change the energy of situations.

I began to weave some of these techniques into my work with clients. The more I was intentional about working for "the highest good of all," and the more I was attentive to my own energy field, the better the results were. Some miraculous things happened. Long-term conflicts were resolved. Immovable barriers dissolved. Seemingly impossible community dreams were achieved.

I didn't talk about the "invisible" work I did. I didn't want my clients to think I was flaky. However, a few people noticed and commented. I began to wish I could be more explicit about my invisible work.

Then I got a project whose clients were open to using meditation and spiritual practices as part of the project work. The project turned out magnificently. Another project provides a similar opportunity.

With our clients, we set our intentions for each stage of the project. We go into a meditative state. We express gratitude for the abundance of help we've received. We visualize the path of the project being easy, smooth and joyful. We state our intention that the project will serve the highest good of those it intends to serve. We become open to inner wisdom.

We close the office door while we do this spiritual work, but we do it.

These projects connect my two work worlds—traditional consulting work, and spiritual work. I'm filled with gratitude.

That brings me to what I consider the greatest gift of being an entrepreneur. As I change, the entrepreneur venture can change too. I get to make it up as I go along.

Re-align the purpose

When I first began the business I didn't think about a larger purpose. I just wanted to escape a soul-destroying job… and I did.

As time went on, I defined the business purpose as two-fold: to serve my clients and to earn a living… and I did.

As I got more successful, I still wanted the business to serve my clients. I also wanted the business not only to earn a living, but to create the life I wanted… and it did.

I'm re-framing my business purpose again. I still want it to serve clients and create the life I want, but now I understand a third business purpose: to be a vehicle for contributing my unique gifts to the planet.

I wouldn't say this just anywhere, but in a book called *Power and Soul,* it seems appropriate. I am now ready to acknowledge my power; to honor my responsibility to express who I really am:

- A soul in progress, a spark of the divine, who has learned lots and wants to share it with other souls in progress;
- The full me—in all my magnificence, delighting in helping others discover and share their full magnificence.

Being an entrepreneur allows me to do that.

As I'm clear on my intention, things fall into place. Help shows up. Learning is offered on a platter. Opportunities present themselves.

Love, money, expertise, laughter, learning. A joyful life. I have that.

Am I satisfied? Yes and no. Yes, I love my life. No, I don't think it's forever.

One day I'll say, "This is nice. But I'd like this new experience… less of…   more of…"

That will be perfect too.

Advice

Here's what I'd say to a new entrepreneur:

1. Set your intention.
2. Learn all you can, get help, dive in, immerse yourself, and then…
3. Let go. Leave room for magic.
4. Be prepared to keep changing your business as you change and grow.

About the Author:

Bonnie Hutchinson *went from a soul-destroying job, to scraping by as a solo entrepreneur, to creating a six-figure income and a life she loves. She'd love to show you how to use soul power to create the life of your dreams. Free special report:* "How to use soul power to create a life of prosperity, passion and purpose, and contribute the unique gifts that only you can give the world." *Go to* www.soulpowerhome.com. *Contact Bonnie at* bonnie@soulpowerhome.com *Phone 780-429-3369.*

CHAPTER 18

How Willing Are You to Have it All?

Sandor Kovacs

I was 34 years old, standing on a stage in front of 150 people, getting coached by a professional trainer in a personal growth workshop. I was confronting the direction I needed to take to love my life again. I stood there, fearful and ashamed, as the trainer slowly walked down the aisle, asking me -"What have you been doing with your life?"

"I've been traveling the world as a flight attendant, living in Australia and Hawaii for work, and spending the winter months in Winter Park, Colorado, skiing."

"How long have you been doing that?" he asked.

"12 years," I replied.

"You have really been screwing around with your life, haven't you?" he challenged.

"Yes," I said, as tears entered my eyes.

"What do you want to do with your life?" he asked.

"I want your job!" Although I didn't see myself capable.

However, just weeks prior, a couple events occurred that started me on a journey…one that would change my life forever.

It was the middle of winter in Colorado and the largest snow storm in years had just fallen. I was with a fellow group of renegade skiers so we were more than delighted about the snow.

Within hours, the news began to spread around that "Topher", short for Christopher, and one of the best skiers in the bunch, had gone missing. By afternoon when he hadn't returned, it became obvious that something serious had happened to him. We gathered over 300 volunteers along with Colorado's mountain rescue and assembled early the following morning to start searching.

While searching the woods for him, I started to wonder, "What am I doing with MY life? I'm so unhappy. Am I ever going to be happy?"

In the Training Room

"So, you want my job? Why?" he asked.

"I want to be a leader. I want to make a difference," I answered.

"What are you upset about?" he asked, noticing more tears gathering in my eyes.

"I don't think I can do it".

"If you don't do it, what will you do, keep screwing around? Maybe it's time you take responsibility for your life. I invite you to choose right now," he said.

"Choose what?" I asked.

"Choose to love your life, or choose to keep doing what you are doing," he laughed.

"I choose to love my life," I declared.

"When will you start doing that?" he asked.

"Right now!"

Searching on the Mountain

By the end of day one, there was no news from anyone searching for Topher. I knew that with sub-zero degree nights our hopes were diminishing, but we would continue searching the next morning.

For the next two days we searched the woods, poking 10 foot long bamboo poles through deep fresh snow around every tree, trying to find Topher. At 4pm on day three, the mountain rescue team packed up. We all looked at each other with deep despair. We knew Topher was gone. We all decided to ski down except for his best friend Dan.

Dan said to us as he pointed, "I'm going to ski around that way. I'll meet you on the cat walk."

Dan took off around the knoll to the left and we all skied down to the right and waited at the cat walk.

Suddenly Dan yelled out, "I found him! Oh my God, I found him!"

Dan said that he heard Topher's voice in his head say "I'm over here". Dan skied over to a tree, stuck his pole in the snow and hit Topher's boot. Topher had accidentally fallen upside down into the deep soft snow surrounding a tree, got stuck, and drowned in the snow.

Back to the Training Room

"Sandor, how willing are you to have it all?" the trainer asked.

"Willing!" I shouted.

"What does 'have it all' look like?"

I yelled, "I want to be courageous! I want to see myself taking on my life without wondering if I look like a fool or an idiot! I want to be a LEADER!"

"You have just reinvented your life Sandor. Thank you for having the courage to take responsibility for your life."

As I walked down from the stage, I could feel my blood rushing through my body exactly as it did when I would launch myself off a ski jump. My mind felt like it wanted to explode. I felt ecstatic and terrified, but clear about what I needed to do next.

Over the weeks following, I made some drastic changes. I quit the job that I had been in for 12 years, sold most everything I owned, and hit the road in my jeep. I spent the next four months traveling around the West, visiting friends, exploring new ways of learning including having a Reiki treatment. That experience transformed me and my life forever.

I was lying on the massage table as the Reiki master worked on my body when suddenly Topher appeared in my mind's eye. I thought I was seeing things. He was so beautiful with glowing light all around him. He walked toward me, put his hand on my head and said "I love you and I want you to do something for me."

I started to cry as I was filled with a sense of love. I wondered if I was making this up. I looked around the room. Everything was quiet when suddenly the Reiki master said, "All there is, is love and fear."

"Why did you say that?" I asked.

"I felt it in the room," she said.

As I closed my eyes, Topher began to tell me what he wanted me to do.

He said "Tell Stephanie that I love and forgive her. Tell her to go north and do what she loves. "

"Is this real?" I said.

"Yes, it is. I love you Sandor. Tell her that when she does what she loves to do, she needs to wear this."

Toffer held up a pinkish sweatshirt. "Tell her to wear this when she is doing what she loves, but she will need to wash it before wearing it, as it is dirty."

 I thought to myself, that he would never have worn that. He was too cool." Am I making this up?" I asked.

"No, Sandor. You are not." He smiled at me, took his hand off my head, and walked away.

That day happened to be Good Friday.

The next day, even though hesitant in telling Stephanie that I had just spoken with her dead boyfriend, I made the phone call. I explained my entire experience from the search for Topher in the woods to the Reiki treatment. "He wants you to know that he loves you and forgives you," I said.

Through tears, she said, "Oh my God, do you know what happened the morning he died? Topher and I had a fight before he went skiing. He decided to come home to tell me he loved me and make up. I wouldn't listen so he went back to the mountain to ski. Oh God, that was the last time I saw him."

"Well he also wants you to start doing what you love. Do you know what that is?"

"Yes, to be a writer. I have been planning on moving so I could write."

"He wants you to move north. I am not sure why" I said.

"I am considering moving to Alaska. Sandor, this is so strange. Why did he come to you? Why did he not come to me?" she said.

I had no idea.

"I have one other thing to tell you and it is going to sound strange. He wants you to wear a piece of clothing when you write. It is a pinkish sweatshirt. I can't imagine Topher owning something like that."

"I can't think of him wearing that either."

"Wait a minute," she said. "I will be right back." She came back a few moments later. "I have it! It was in the closet. It is all wrinkled and dirty so I will have to wash it before wearing it!"

I gasped and started to cry.

I realized that I had spent my life closed off to new possibilities. I had become cynical and resigned and I realized why Topher picked me. I said that I wanted to make a difference and here was my first opportunity. I suddenly felt so free and so alive. I had spent my life believing that I knew everything and had life all figured out. In an instant, I felt at peace and completely humbled.

We talked a little longer and said our good byes. I later heard that she moved to Alaska to write and follow her dreams.

People have asked me, "What happened to you that winter that gave you the courage to create a new life?"

I told them that I learned courage is not about being 'macho' but about allowing yourself to "be with" fear and commit to moving forward anyway. I learned the real meaning of commitment, personal responsibility and accountability. I learned that what I had interpreted as fear when I thought about changing my life was not fear at all. It was excitement! My soul was starving for me to live a different life. I realized that Topher's death was his gift to me.

So I took off for San Francisco in my Jeep with just my clothes and my bicycle to begin a new life. A life made by design and not by circumstance. I was happy for the first time in a very long while.

About the Author:

Fast forward to today... **Sandor Kovacs** *is the CEO of* RunRhino™, *which specializes in executive coaching, management consulting, leadership retreats, and customized trainings, focusing on people achieving extraordinary success, while expressing their true passion in life. Sandor enjoys life in Santa Cruz, Calif. with his wife Joy and their 5-year-old son Phoenix. For more information on RunRhino, Sandor's story, newsletter, and to receive lessons Sandor has learned in the years since this story took place, visit* www.runrhino.com

CHAPTER 19

5 Steps to Living the Life of Your Dreams: Dreams Do Come True!

Diana Long

I have had a lifelong fascination with dreams coming true. As a young girl I had an unlikely "role" model. I was enthralled with the lovely, magical and powerful Samantha, portrayed by actress Elizabeth Montgomery, on the TV series, *Bewitched*. My secret wish was that I too could wrinkle and twinkle up my nose and make amazing things happen around me! I wanted to be empowered to create and manifest my own dreams and have fun doing it. For over 30 years I have followed this intense inner desire and have studied and trained extensively with masters in the field of personal development, human potential and success technology.

In my "previous" work life, I worked as Licensed Professional Counselor for over a decade. At the time my personal life went through several shifts and turns including ending a 7 year long marriage (which produced my handsome son, Justin). I suddenly became a single parent raising and supporting a child on my own. Within a couple of years (and by using the "power of intention"), I met my incredibly, supportive current husband of 17 years. In a whirlwind of romance and trips to exotic locations, we were married. Nine months later, we welcomed our beautiful daughter, Emily. For several years, I was a devoted "stay-at-home" mom. I thoroughly enjoyed this "gig" but as my children grew, I felt an inner urge to return to the working world. To my astonishment, my desire to work as a counselor no longer had the appeal that it once had for me. I was at a crossroads. I hired a Success Coach to help me to discover what was next for me. I quickly realized what I wanted to do…to Coach! I discovered a passion to coach women entrepreneurs who are conscious, creative and have a burning desire to live their life to the absolute fullest!

As a result of years of study, practice and coaching others, I created a 5 step system that will help you to design and live the life of your dreams (and Samantha's nose wrinkling and twinkling technique is completely optional!)

Step # 1 "Start with What You Don't Want"

Yes, you heard that correctly! It may seem counterintuitive but it is actually very valuable for us to start exactly where you are right now—including the "good, the bad, and the ugly".

It's crucial for us to acknowledge this place where you are now and to take responsibility for it.

1. Maybe you are dissatisfied with how much money you earn relative to how much you work.

2. Perhaps you woke up this morning and realized that you are filled with dread about working one more day at your current job. It's a moment of Truth.

3. Or maybe you have BIG dreams about what is possible for you, but you feel frustrated, overwhelmed and unsure about how you can really make it happen.

We have to be honest with ourselves before we can move forward. From this point of contrast, you are then able to clarify what you really do want and begin to shift your focus.

Too much of our precious time and energy is spent complaining and being unhappy about our current situation. We can easily get stuck here if we aren't proactive. Here's the secret: Use your "frustration or "unhappiness" as information that you will use as a springboard to learn what you do want.

Here's what I'd suggest you do: Write down a list of all the things that you have right now that you don't want. Next to every item, write down the *antidote*, in other words what you really want. This leads us to Step #2...

Step #2 "Dare to Dream Big!"

Give yourself permission to expose your hearts truest desires. Open up the door of possibilities for yourself. Many of us, as "mature" adults have become too realistic. We've become caught up in all the things we feel we "should" be doing on our endless 'To-Do' List

So I ask you... Are you living life? Or is life living you? How compelling is your life? Do you wake up in the morning excited to jump out of bed and get your day started?

If you answered "yes", fantastic! You are definitely on the fast track of success. If you answered, "No way! I can barely get out of bed each morning" or "Thank God for the snooze alarm", then I'm telling you—get excited about your life again! What do you *really* want and why? Spend some quality time with yourself ASAP brainstorming all the things you would love to do, to be, to experience in your lifetime so that when it is all over and done you can honestly say that you lived your life to the fullest. Write down all of your wonderful ideas. Nothing is off limits. Don't worry about how you are going to make it happen. Just let yourself reconnect with your dreams and your dreams will show you who you really are!

Remember, life gives us what we ask of it. Let's ask for what we want. Why settle for less?

Step #3 "Declare Your Desire!"

Did you know that your thoughts have tremendous power? By using the power of your thoughts and creating statements of intention you will create results. Have you ever noticed that people who speak about great health, prosperity, and gratitude are healthy, prosperous and positive people and that those who tell a story of all the things that are going wrong with them, their poor health, their shaky relationships, their lack of money tend to continue to have more and more of these negative circumstances in their lives? The law of attraction is very simple. Life attracts like. We attract to us what we think most about. Thoughts become things.

Speak more of what you do want and less and less about what you don't want. To utilize this power of Step 3, Declare Your Desire, simply write down your intentions for all the arenas of your life. What do you intend to have in the areas of personal finances…your family…your career goals… your health and wellness…your sense of adventure and travel… your spirituality…

You get the idea! I guarantee that you will be fired up once you've created your list of your own specific intentions. Powerful stuff!

Step #4 "Own Your Vision"

What you can believe, you can achieve!

Now that you have declared your desires and created your own list of powerful intentions, let's take it to the next level and "Turbo-charge" your own vision of success with step #4, which is Owning Your Vision".

We need to "visualize" in order to "materialize".

Star Athletes, top performing artists, and CEO's know and use this secret step of visualization. Those at the top of their 'game' use the power of their imagination to mentally rehearse their dreams and goals into fruition. They see themselves winning the race, putting large checks into their bank account and closing the big sale.

What are your dreams and goals? Its time for you to "own your vision". I recommend that you spend 5-10 minutes twice a day (more if you can), daydreaming about a highly desired dream of yours. Get comfy in a soft chair, close your eyes and picture everything going exactly the way you'd like it to be in your mind's eye. Really get into it- feel it - see it - touch it - taste it. Really and truly experience it.

Faithfully "own your vision" each and every day. Visualize your goals with positive powerful emotion and you'll be amazed how quickly things will begin to line up for you!

Step #5 "Just Do It"

Just Do IT! Now it's time to take action. Did you know that out of a 100 people, approximately 67% of the 100 have goals? Out of those 67%, approximately 10% have their goals written down on paper. Of those 10%, approximately 2% actually achieve their goals. Rather sobering statistics, aren't they? My wish for you? I want you to be one of the 2%! What the folks in this group did differently was to create a step by step plan of action to get their goals met.

It can be easy to get "fired" up after listening to a motivational program and attempt to overachieve and try to do too many things at once. My recommendation is for you to pick your top 3 priorities. Name your goals, write them down and then step by step map out what needs to happen next. Then take the necessary actions, step by step, day by day, to begin to live your dreams! Just do it!

That's it. 5 simple, yet incredibly potent steps that will take you into the direction of your wildest dreams. Bon voyage!

About the Author:

Success Coach and Speaker, **Diana Long***, is the President of the* Life Design Institute. *Diana can help you transform your dreams into reality and give you the shortcuts to success with a variety of life-changing programs and products.*

To learn more about Diana and receive your Free Report, How to Avoid the 3 Biggest Mistakes that Women Make to Sabotage their Success *plus Free subscription to* Life Design Secrets *e-newsletter, please* visit www.DianaLong.com

CHAPTER 20

Life Lessons From a Starlet's Dressing Room

Liz Pabon, "The Branding Maven"

Free yourself from the #1 obstacle that gets in the way of discovering your greatness.

There it was, just sitting there perfectly polished, a classic but with an unusual twist you couldn't quite put your finger on. Wearing it made me feel strong, powerful and safe. It commanded attention, respect and earned great acclaim—a perfect accessory by anyone's definition. The trouble was the fit was all wrong.

A Fading Star

Sitting in my corporate ivory tower, overlooking the San Francisco bay, I asked myself why I wasn't satisfied. I had a fantastic job, more than enough money in the bank, my own home and a shoe collection that would make Imelda Marcos cry.

For weeks I watched my days pass before me as though I were an outsider looking in—a stranger in my own life. Every meeting, phone call, and encounter felt as though I were unraveling a riddle that was difficult to solve—I needed my 'bat senses' engaged... and quick!

Then one day, it finally dawned on me. I had lost myself in the promotions; the trips across the country; the meetings over elaborate dinners, and the process of moving up the ladder. I had climbed so high that I quite literally left my most favorite accessory, an original, behind. Me.

Not one that needs to be hit over the head twice, I knew it was time to write a new script for my life. So, donning my stilettos and designer bag, I strutted my way out of one world—ready—exit stage left—to take the entrepreneurial world by storm. If I could succeed in the corporate world, entrepreneurship would surely be a breeze. Or so I thought.

Auditioning

Launching my small business was exciting. I applied all my business savvy, created a business plan, researched my market—I left nothing to chance. Off I went to tell the world what I did and why I was the best and only choice.

As I started mixing and mingling something didn't feel right. At the end of each day I felt out of sorts, uncomfortable. You know the feeling. Similar to a great pair of shoes, gorgeous in fact, but they're only good for sitting and perhaps making a short obligatory stroll across the room. Well, that's what I felt like and I couldn't explain why.

Fast-forward one year. My business was doing fine but as an over-achiever (believe me when I tell you that's a huge understatement), fine wasn't good enough. Then I hit a wall. Slammed into it is a more appropriate description.

I suffered a depression I'd never experienced before. The kind that makes you crawl out of bed meekly and even the most gorgeous new pair of designer strappy sandals can't resuscitate the life back into you. Can you relate?

After lots of soul searching I realized that while I was follow-ing my dream of entrepreneurship and empowering women to tap into their inner star power, I had forgotten to tap into mine. I was so eager to jump into the entrepreneurial world that I didn't take time out to make an internal assessment of my absolute most valued product, the product that would ultimately attract the kind of success I sought—me.

When I stopped long enough to take a peek under the hood, I realized that leaving the corporate world to pursue my dream of running my own business was just a first step. There was so much more involved in creating a wildly successful business that went beyond creating a well-organized business plan.

You see, what I discovered during my "don't want to wash my hair" depressive haze was that I wasn't connecting the core of who I was with my audience in the most meaningful way. As a personal brand strategist, I committed a huge faux pas. I voraciously launched my new business as "corporate Liz" and didn't realize that it was 'she', the accessory that served me so well in years past, that no longer fit.

So, the task of letting go of "corporate Liz" stood before me like a huge clearance bin—one you know you've got to sift through (junk and all), in order to find that great designer treasure buried below.

Letting go of a persona that served me so well, protected, shielded and helped me survive my past and brought me great success, was a little scary. Okay, it was very scary. Slowly, I began the process of letting go and getting out of my own way so that I could walk down life's runway, in the way I was intended. It's this process that I now lovingly refer to as getting into the Wild Success Zone™:

DRESSING ROOM CLEAN OUT!

This wouldn't be a proper success formula if it didn't include recognizing the time is right. Clients I work with often say they don't know why after 10+ years they suddenly feel what once worked, no longer does. I explain to them that they are growing, evolving and the persona that once served them so well no longer fits. Give yourself permission to accept this realization.

All around me I saw movement—life at full speed. It was not until I slowed down during my depressive fog that I became conscious of the persona I had to let go of and the woman whose birth I was responsible for.

I won't lie to you. In many ways it felt like a part of me had died (parts of me did), and I grieved that loss at my deepest core. Today, "corporate Liz" is a fond memory. I honor who she was and what she gave me. Without her strength (a trait I still carry today) to support me I might have never made this incredible voyage.

The Fitting Room

Imagine yourself a tailor, pulling, tugging and pinning your favorite garment for that most perfect fit. The process of getting out of your own way means you'll have to pull, tug and possibly nip at some of the behaviors, habits, and thought processes that worked for you in years past but will no longer support you on the rest of your journey.

During my passage in the Wild Success Zone™, I discovered that I had to release myself from the bondage of my own thinking. It was this letting go that awakened in me the woman I was destined to become. Up until then, I was asleep to who I was and to achieving my greatest potential.

Rumor Control

One day you look in the mirror and what stares back at you is your most amazing self. Let me share that I personally never felt more free than when I stepped out of the fitting room (being in there was no fun…those lights, eek!), and emerged a starlet.

Although you are feeling more confident and more sure of your purpose than you ever imagined, it may come as a surprise when those around you aren't as excited about your rebirth.

Know that your light, shining so brightly now, will make some people uncomfortable. Be prepared to say "ta, ta" if necessary because your greatness is NOT negotiable. Make no mistake about it—you are destined for super stardom. Beware of those that try to keep you in your old clothes. In fact, do them a favor and hand them a pair of shades. They'll need something to protect their eyes from your blinding light!

A Star is Born!

They say that no one is perfect and expecting perfection is futile. I have to disagree. Perfection lies within all of us. It's our definition of perfection that's a bit out of whack. True success starts inside of you. Discovering and coming to terms with your unique gifts, talents, quirks, everything that makes you a true collector's item is the first step towards your own one-of-a-kind perfection.

Each and every one of you reading these words is worthy of walking down your own red carpet. Sometimes however, we need a little help with hair and makeup. That's why I developed the *Creating Wild Success Circle of Stars*, a mastermind program for women that wish to unlock their inner star power.

Life Lessons

What I've learned and know for certain is that until you look yourself fully under life's dressing room lights, and recognize your inner star power you are placing limits on your potential.

You don't have to travel down the Wild Success Zone™ alone. The Circle of Stars surrounds you to help you twinkle a little brighter and bring you up to a whole new level of stardom. It is my great passion and purpose to lead you down the path towards your ultimate greatness.

Success is possible, no matter what you've been told or what you've told yourself. *Creating Wild Success Circle of Stars* is the perfect pit stop for sky rocketing your success and blasting you into a whole new orbit. Don't worry, no paparazzos allowed!

Dedicated to my beautiful friend, and kindred spirit Adriana Dontje, whose star will always shine bright. Until we see one another again. XO

About the Author:

Liz Pabon, *"The Branding Maven," is inspiring, motivating and empowering—but most importantly, she's effective. Liz publishes the playful and insightful,* **Keys 2 Wild Success!** *ezine. Get ready to develop a personal brand that brings you star power, has raving fans clamoring to work with you, and makes you more money while having lots more FUN in your small business. Visit* www.thebrandingmaven.com *to get your FREE Wild Success tips today.*

CHAPTER 21

Chase Your Dreams:
Stay the Course

ARTHUR REGO

"Dream lofty dreams, and as you dream so shall you become. Your vision is the promise of what you shall at last unveil."

— John Ruskin

CHASE YOUR DREAMS

I am building a successful online and offline business with a proven system and sharing it with others, showing people that with the right effort and good advice, they too can realize their dreams.

You too can make your dreams come true. It won't be easy, but with goals, a carefully considered plan, and the right attitude, you can realize all of your dreams.

"What is a dream? Your dream is that idea, that vision for your life, which burns inside of you. It keeps coming back to your mind because it is part of who you are; it will never leave you alone."

— From *Reaching Your Dreams* by Tommy Barnett.

In order to succeed, I had to decide to take control of my life and fight for my financial freedom. The process required me to decide what was really important to me and to integrate the desired outcomes into my thinking.

So you already know what your dreams are. They're the ones that keep coming back to you when the little voice in the back of your mind, the you that you could be, speaks.

To succeed, you need to know first what it is you hope to achieve. Do not set yourself some vague goals, like "Make money and be happy." Everyone wants that, but wanting is not doing, and succeeding requires doing.

Set yourself some specific targets, and then start out in that direction. Always keep your eyes and ears open to what is happening around you, but stay true to your purpose and your goal.

Create milestones so that you can judge your progress. The better you plan, the more successful the chase will be. Dreams arise spontaneously; everything else is in the planning.

> *"The purpose of a dream is to focus our attention. The mind will not reach for achievement until it has clear objectives. The magic begins when we own our dream. It is then that the switch is turned on, the current begins to flow, and the power to accomplish becomes a reality."*
>
> — Author unknown

Successful people appreciate the accomplishments of others. A key decision I made early was to seek out and listen to spiritual and business mentors. For while no one has ever been you, or dreamed your dreams, others have succeeded, just as you will. Success is a universal process. Only the details are personal.

> *"Inspiration to action is the most important ingredient of success in any human activity. And inspiration to action can be developed at will."*
>
> — W. Clement Stone

Above all else: no matter whom you are or what you want to achieve, you must focus on a plan. Think before you act. Plan before you execute. And then, no matter what else may happen, no matter what distractions may present themselves (and present themselves they will) you must stay the course.

Stay The Course

Here are seven keys to staying the course.
1. Your quest and the pursuit of your dream calls for great determination and drive.
2. Develop a "never quit" mindset. The key to not quitting is to forge ahead with the strength and vision of an eagle, no matter what life throws at you.
3. Develop and maintain a razor sharp focus.
4. Couple a warrior-like spirit with great faith and expectations.
5. Think and operate outside the box.
6. Be persistent and always keep the end in view.
7. Believe in yourself and set no limits on what you can achieve.

No meaningful progress is ever made without overcoming obstacles. In my life, I had a major financial challenge to overcome, that at times threatened to overwhelm me. You may know (in fact you must know), exactly what it is that you want to achieve, but you should also know that the road to success will have curves and bumps and potholes. If you know they're coming, dealing with them is much easier.

> *"I have found that success is measured not so much by the position attained in life, as by the obstacles that have been overcome in attaining that position."*
> — Dr. Booker T. Washington

As I was racing down the path I had chosen, I also had to face discouragement and doubt from others. You know exactly what I mean. It's your dream. Other people didn't have that dream, and they might not understand what you know. I overcame these problems through a combination of my faith, by reading books on great leadership, and by surrounding myself with people who were "overcomers".

You have to stick to it, come what may.

"Continuous effort, not strength or intelligence, is the key to unlocking your potential."

— Winston Churchill

Here are seven obstacles that you might encounter:
1. Doubting yourself and your God-given abilities.
2. Listening to unsuccessful people who have no "fruit on the tree".
3. Placing limitations on your goals, dreams and hopes.
4. Allowing others to steal your dreams.
5. Not acting on your dreams once you have identified them and a timetable by which to achieve them.
6. Giving up before you have reached your goal or achieved your dreams.
7. Giving into a mindset that says: "I guess it was not meant to be".

"Your rewards in life are determined by the problems you are willing to solve for others."
— From *The Wisdom Commentary* by Mike Murdock

Personal and business success requires change. I had to replace small and negative thinking with a larger, more positive outlook; learn to operate outside my comfort zone; ignore the doubters; and replace the average with the excellent. There is no room for selfish thinking, doubt, or excuses. What is needed is a "can do" attitude, which many people think they have, but find, in practice, that they cannot summon.

"Many people fail in life because they believe in the adage: 'If

you don't succeed, try something else.' But success eludes those who follow such advice. The dreams that came true did so because people stuck to their ambitions. They refused to be discouraged. They never let disappointment get the upper hand. Challenges only spurred them on to greater efforts."

— Don B. Owens, Jr

Succeeding is about building long-term relationships. Success is about making a difference in the lives of many people, of which you are merely one. You will succeed by changing the environment in which all those you deal with are able to succeed. A river flows in one direction and everything in it flows in that direction.

> *"There is no more noble occupation in the world, than to assist another human being and to help someone succeed."*

— Alan Loy McGinnis

Here are seven attributes associated with success:

1. A focus on helping others realize their dreams that, in turn, leads to achieving your own dreams.
2. A consistently upbeat attitude, even (and especially), in the valley of adversity.
3. Surrounding yourself with extremely successful people and seeking their counsel.
4. Chasing your dreams with relentless focus and never allowing others to distract you.
5. Creating options and opportunities for yourself and others.
6. Smart thinking followed by the rapid implementation of plans and ideas.
7. Successful people are competitors, not spectators.

Not everyone has other people's best interests at heart. Not everyone is driven to make the connections necessary for success. Most of all, I know that to succeed, you must help others to achieve their goals and dreams. Service to others is not just a buzzword; it lies at the heart of every success story.

"One of the marks of successful people is that they are action-oriented. One of the marks of average people is that they are talk-oriented."

— Brian Tracy

Chase your dreams with relentless passion and persistence. Stay the course, which means never, ever, giving up or quitting. If circumstances force you to think about quitting, because it seems like the easier course of action, remember that quitting is not action; it is inaction.

"I do not think that there is any other quality so essential to success of any kind as the quality of perseverance. It overcomes almost everything, even nature."

— J.D. Rockefeller

STAY THE COURSE.

Your peers, friends and associates will not judge you by how you started, but by how you finished the race called life.

"Destiny is not a matter of chance; it is a matter of choice. It is not a thing to be waited for; it is a thing to be achieved."

—From *Focus on Your Dream* by Jeffrey Smith

Your attitude dictates your destiny. Set out to succeed, focus on your dreams, never say die, and you will succeed.

About the Author:

Arthur Rego *is President of AER Enterprises, which operates several busi-nesses, including* Wellness for Life. *He helps individuals in their search for optimal health, using a proven and safe wellness system. He is also a motivational speaker. Strong leadership and strong values, he believes, is the recipe for a strong country. Arthur and his wife Ann live in Bermuda and have two children, Alison and Arthur Jr., and three grandchildren, Abigail, Nathan and Jonah. He can be reached via* arego@northrock.bm, www.arego.qhealthbeauty.com *or 441-505-2260.*

CHAPTER 22

From Pitiful to Powerful— How a Southern Woman Went From Struggling People Pleaser to Successful Business Woman at 50

Cookie Tuminello

"I don't know the key to success, but the key to failure is trying to please everybody."

—Bill Cosby

As women we all struggle with being people pleasers, but as Southern women your worth is measured by it. I think it's a gene we get at birth. Add to that, my full-blooded Italian, Catholic roots and you have a 'gotta feel guilty to feel good' double whammy.

Don't get me wrong, I'm very proud of my heritage. I come from a very close knit, passionate, Italian Catholic family that I dearly love. However, because I was taught to be a nurturer and server from birth, it took me a lot longer (50 years to be exact), to figure out what I wanted and where I was going.

Like many Italian girls, I married early at age 19. Two children and 11 years later, I was divorced, dazed, and feeling like a failure. With a family to support, I got a job and started over. Five years later, I met and married the man of my dreams. After only 14 months of wedded bliss, I unexpectedly became a young widow at 36. Even though I was numb with grief, giving up was not an option. Unfortunately, I knew this scenario well. My mother had become a widow at 46.

After several attempts to find my place, I started my own image consulting business. After many years of burying myself in my work and family, I began to question a lot of things in my life.

A friend knew I was struggling and suggested I attend a personal development workshop with her. My life was changed forever. The defining moment for me was when the coach asked me to stop and 'check in'—I thought he meant the hotel. I had no idea I'd been living my life so cluelessly and unconsciously. I finally got "it". And "it" was three powerful revelations. They were…

1. I had choices.
2. I had to please myself first before I could please others.
3. I had to take back my power.

As a result of these amazing revelations, I climbed out of the deep hole I had dug for myself. I became a coach and started my own company at 50. Some of us take a little longer than others to get "it".

After I took that first big step, I thought, 'Okay, Now what?'

The problem with people pleasing is that it's woven into the fabric of your life and into the expectations of others. Once you make the choice to climb out of that deep, dark hole, the universe is going to challenge you every day to see if you're really serious. Even though I was considered a gutsy Southern lady, people pleasing had diminished me. It had squelched my passion, my power, my purpose, and my dreams. Most importantly, it had taken away my precious freedom.

The time had come for me to reclaim the pieces of myself that I'd given away throughout my life. It was time to take back my power.

Joseph Campbell said it very eloquently, *"We must be willing to give up the life we've planned, to have the life that's waiting for us."*

I now had to identify the "it" that was holding me back. "It" was…

- I was afraid to ask for what I wanted.
- I was afraid to say "No".
- I was afraid to set boundaries.
- I was afraid to charge more for my services.

And why was I so afraid?

Well, my history, my traditions, and my parents had taught me well how to be seen and not heard—"Yes Ma'am, Yes Sir." Now I had to risk not being liked. To illustrate, when I started my coaching business, it was suggested that I use my given name, Beverly, because it sounded more professional than Cookie. And of course, believing others knew more than I did, I acquiesced. After about a year, I was having a major identity crisis with the name thing. I had been nicknamed "Cookie" since birth and that's all anyone had ever called me and I liked it. I decided to risk not being liked. Hence, *Success Source* was born, featuring yours truly, Cookie Tuminello, Success Coach. AH, I felt whole again. And off I went to claim my place as a successful business woman and help other Southern women do the same.

The good news about climbing out of the people pleasing hole and up the ladder of success is that the more you apply what you learn, the more you grow, and the more confident you become.

I learned that the difference between success and merely surviving was the ability to discover and recognize my own core values (those things I hold most dear), and then integrate them into every aspect of my personal and professional life.

Remember my first two revelations? Well, this brings me to my third revelation:

Owning The Power Within.

What a revelation finally waking up and realizing I had all the tools I needed to be successful right inside of me. I just needed to learn how to use them. What a relief! I thought that was a gene I didn't get at birth.

The Buddhists have a saying, "In the beginner's mind there are many possibilities, in the expert's mind there are few."

The idea behind this philosophy is that in order to make changes in your life you must first empty your mind of old beliefs so that you can make room for new possibilities.

Each year I start off with a theme and a commitment declaration. This practice keeps me on track and honors my intentions.

You notice I said commitment. For me, there's a big difference between setting a goal and being committed to something. I say the difference is that commitment comes from within and goals are the action steps that get you there.

In order to fulfill my commitment to myself, I had to be willing to submit myself to the process of change and get support. Yes, coaches have coaches. I don't ask my clients to go anywhere I haven't been or am willing to go.

Here are the 7 Success Strategies that I now use to coach other women to think bigger and bolder about themselves and create the life they want and deserve now.

1. DETERMINE WHERE YOU'RE GOING AND WHAT YOU WANT. You can't get there if you don't know where you are going. Otherwise, how will you know when you get there? Be specific. Write it down. Make a plan to get it. Need guidance? Check out Henriette Klauser's book, *Write it down, Make it happen.*

2. DETERMINE WHAT'S WORKING AND WHAT'S NOT WORKING IN YOUR LIFE. How many of your current life choices reflect your core values? How many are "shoulds" and how many are "choices"? Core values are the foundation for who you are, not who you want to be or whom you think you should be. For example, how many times have you made a decision and after you made that decision, you knew you'd made a mistake? That's probably because your decision was at odds with your core vales. When you live your life out of your core values, you life is permeated with more passion, purpose, and peace.

3. LEARN TO ASK FOR WHAT YOU WANT. Your success is tied to your ability to make effective requests. The more effective

requests you make, the more successful you will be. When you don't ask, you don't get.

4. LEARN HOW TO SAY "NO" AND MEAN IT. Stop trying to be all things to all people. Saying Yes when you want say No drains you of precious energy, causes resentment and lack of commitment. Be careful not to overextend yourself. Set boundaries.

5. TAKE ACTION. Nothing changes until you take action. Remove one at a time, the habits that no longer meet your needs. Your actions have to match your intentions.

6. GET SUPPORT. Support helps you take better care of yourself. You can do it by yourself but committed support gets you there faster. Committed support is someone whose only agenda is to help you get where you want to go. Get a coach if you need one. A coach will keep you focused.

7. BE PATIENT WITH YOURSELF. It takes time, practice, and rigor to change habits that have been around a long time. It's okay to fall down as long as you get back up again.

One thing is for sure: if you begin to change the present, the future will surely be different. Stepping off into the abyss can be scary, but the rewards are well worth the risk. Why settle for half a life when you can have a full life filled with success beyond your wildest dreams?

About the Author:

Cookie Tuminello *has been a Business and Personal Success Coach since 1995. Her passion is inspiring and empowering successful women in business to think bigger and bolder about themselves, unleash their full potential, and bridge the gap between their goals and actions. She does individual coaching, workshops, guest speaking, and Management/Leadership trainings. She produces a FREE Inspirational Weekly Ezine called* Monday Morning Coffee With Cookie *which you may subscribe to at* www.cookietuminello.com.

PART III

Success from the Soul

CHAPTER 23

Leading With Your Heart

Marian L. Bayham, CLTC, LTCP, CSA

Imagine a day where your personal autonomy and confident self-reliance has been stripped from you. If you will, let your imagination conjure up this scenario…

An auto accident or, some such malady beyond your control, has left you, a once vibrant, healthy individual, incapacitated. During your recovery, you chance upon that rare opportunity to peer into a mirror and behold a frail individual staring back at you. You don't recognize this person. Once simple tasks such as bathing, dressing, and walking have become feats of endurance and fortitude. What possible thoughts now dance around in your head as this ghost of a former self stares back at you? Is it one of helplessness, sadness, anger, and frustration? Has your reflection asked, "Why me?"

Would you be moved at this juncture in your life to see your future as an endless dreary landscape filled with unrelenting challenges, or as a blank canvas onto which you could paint a new life?

By now, an unspoken thought has probably announced its presence to you with a silent murmur, "Things like this happen to other people." Indeed, many of us would rather not contemplate this ill-fated scenario. However, for many individuals, young and old, this frightening portrayal is already a reality.

Life's Lessons Unannounced

At an unconscious level, we probably accept the notion that "Bad things don't happen to good people."

Well, in my universe, it did. My husband Bill had been enduring a considerable amount of back pain and discomfort for a number of years. It culminated one night with him "wetting the bed." The doctors explained that a herniated disc had put pressure on a nerve to his bladder. If the pressure were not relieved, the damage would be irreversible. Well, we didn't take the thought of surgery lightly. We were assured by the medical specialists that a procedure to alleviate his pain would correct the problem with a better than 95% chance of success. Thus, at the age of 47, my husband was wheeled reluctantly into the operating room.

The surgery provided Bill with a modicum of relief. In fact, the doctors had him walking within a day of his surgery despite his protests. Unbeknownst to us, the universe was about to put Bill through a test of endurance and survival.

It was less than a week after I had brought Bill home from the hospital and I was enjoying a quiet Sunday morning with my own thoughts. I noticed that Bill appeared to be softly moaning in his sleep. Upon reaching over to caress his forehead, I knew something was definitely wrong. As the minutes passed, my worry grew with the intensity of Bill's discomfort. The sudden onset of his intense pain and his final scream, "I'm on fire!" threw me into action.

The paramedics arrived within minutes after my call. Bill was screaming in agony as he was transferred to the gurney and then to the ambulance. The attending physician informed me that Bill's white blood cell count was dangerously low and that a severe infection was raging throughout his body.

I learned that Bill's infection had been contracted during his hospital stay. A virulent bacterial infection was now consuming his spinal cord. The infection nearly took his life. After 28 days in the hospital, 6 months of home care and rehabilitation, and months learning to walk, he swears he will never go near a hospital again.

This experience provided me with an 'in-your-face' encounter with the limits of medicine and reinforced for me, the powers of faith, compassion, endurance, and a giving heart. Without ever knowing how or why, the life I had generally taken for granted had suddenly made a U-turn. I had been presented with a ringside seat to care giving, 24/7, along with its ensuing physical and mental demands. Life wasn't as secure as I had accustomed myself to believe.

Upon some reflection, I've come to recognize that in addition to my career, the care of my husband during his recovery has been my most challenging, most demanding, and, yet, in some strange fashion, most rewarding.

POLLYANNA FINDS A CAREER IN SALES

Although Bill had dodged his grim reaper, a nagging thought continued to linger at the back of my mind, "What if he had not recovered? What if he had needed care for the rest of his life? What if…what if?" Although, as a couple, we had prepared for such an eventuality, its occurrence continued to haunt me.

In my role as a *Long Term Care Insurance* agent, I consult with clients who initially don't see a need for my products or services. "That will never happen to me!" is a refrain I hear often. They have never consciously asked themselves "what if…. "

Denial takes many forms and this happens to be one of its many guises. Because the idea of needing long-term care is so foreign to many individuals, they ignore its overall consequences. Its impact on health, family, finances, lifestyle, career, and relationships are the sultry effects of denial, complacency, fear, and ignorance.

You might then ask me, "How do you succeed in such a business?" I'll simply reply, "Lead with your heart, and everything else will fall into place." Surviving in an industry with an 85% agent turnover may make my response seem Pollyannaish, but today's business climate demands something more of us than a great idea or superior product.

BELIEVE EVERYTHING IS POSSIBLE

Do you remember the children's story about the little railroad engine that puffed, "I think I can—I think I can—I think I can," as it pulled a train of freight cars up a long grade? Do you recall your delight as the little engine topped the hill announcing in loud triumphant puffs for all to hear, "I thought I could—I thought I could—I thought I could."

How often do we limit what we can do by the simple words, "I can't?" By refusing to be chained by what we think is possible, and insisting on the impossible by saying, "I can," permits us the freedom to eventually say to the world, "I thought I could!"

LEAD WITH YOUR HEART

My 'Pollyanna' allows me to believe that "I can." My business is not about selling insurance, but about helping people. I coined the phrase *"Leading With Your Heart"* to remind myself of the fact that my major competition has not been other agents, but my own fears and self-doubts. So this is where "heart" comes into play. Simply put, it means connecting to others in a way that nourishes them emotionally and spiritually. It is the moral equivalent of fertilizer for my business. I've found this to be especially true when promoting long-term care insurance products, which are often viewed as unnecessary.

PLAYING MY WAY TO SUCCESS

I learned at a very early age while working in my parent's bakery that chores had a nasty habit of taking me away from my playtime. I discovered to my amazement that by strategically planning my day, I could, in fact, increase my playtime.

Those who succeed in life are no smarter, nor more talented than me, was my thought as a child – they just had a better plan of action. Now, as a successful entrepreneur, my beliefs are supercharged by a strong work ethic, a willingness to take risks, and the wherewithal to persevere. Wanting more playtime had indirectly taught me about goal setting.

Playground Rules

Creating new ways to educate more people about the importance of long-term care in order to preserve lifestyles and hard-earned monies has become my new playground. My playtime is now mapped to a 'Plan of Action' based on my belief that long-term dreams are attained by making short hops to more attainable goals—sort of like a game of hopscotch. Before I cast my hopscotch pebble, my 'Pollyanna' reminds me to always play all-out, to help my fellow players improve their game, to laugh at myself, and to have fun.

A Time for Reflection

Just as playing the same game can be boring after awhile; complacency in one's life can lead to an atrophy of ambition. I continuously reinvent my game of hopscotch, always asking myself, "How can my services have the most positive impact on people's lives?"

Pushing the change envelope is refreshing. It permits me to uncover new opportunities while at the same time keeping me humble when my ideas end up on the scrap heap. The child within me always wants to play with the next new game. Whether successful or not, she's gained self-confidence just from the trying. The game-of-life has been a masterful coach.

A GRATEFUL HEART

My views on success are not something you haven't read before, it's just a different script with a new set of characters. Just as the little railroad engine announced, "I thought I could," the manifestation of your plans into action will inspire your imagination to propel you forward.

Permit yourself to engage the world with a grateful heart and be touched, moved, and inspired by your own uniqueness. May your blessings be realized in the unseen events of your life. Go forth and live that life of significance, which in my universe means, "giving back" some of the abundance you have reaped.

About the Author:

Marian L. Bayham *is "Your Long Term Care Specialist for Life." She helps to educate consumers about the devastating financial and psychological impacts of long-term care. Helping families make well-informed choices and unconditional respect for clients motivate her. Marian can advise you about protecting your lifestyle and retirement portfolio while preserving your dignity and independence. She represents several companies and is licensed in most states. For a free consultation, contact Marian at 866-826-3582 or visit* www.lovinglongtermcare.com.

CHAPTER 24

Life is Beautiful

Dominique Bossavy

This chapter is dedicated to all of those who are seeking a higher purpose.

I was born and raised in a small village of the south Atlantic coast of France, the second of five children, from a middle class family.

Capricious, with big ideas, an innate creative mind, a happy spirit and a fascination for makeup that no one could explain. I took on life with humor and excitement. Rebellious by nature I enjoyed learning on my on terms, preferably outside of the rigid school structure and opposing against parental authority. Thirsting for new experiences, conquering my right for freedom, adventuring and exploring everyday with verve and no regrets for the price to pay—the awaiting punishment for disobeying—and following my creative impulses.

I always refused to conform to conventional and narrow thinking, boldly defying anything that didn't rhyme with freedom of choice. I was worlds away from stereotypes and awarded the infamous title of *black sheep of the family*. This often led to my being told that I was 'stupid', 'good for nothing' and would end up in the local village factory making wooden baskets for strawberries and oysters. However I never believed a word of these labels!

I spent most of my youth surviving what I call " character disfiguration', confronting and battling the 'should's and 'shouldn't's' inflicted upon me by an unrelentingly severe and conservative generation that didn't know better and thought of me as being dysfunctional . Constantly in conflict with my mother at times was very painful. Our misunderstanding of each other was brutal, and my heart was frequently shredded to pieces by her harsh comments and slapping hand's. I often felt very disconnected and lonely.

As time went by, my mother's temper escalated out of proportion. Without notice, out of the blue, she arranged to take me to an orphanage called *"The Castle of La Tifardiere.*" What I thought was going to be a treat by visiting a castle and meet new friends to play with, turned into cold abandonment. My mother left me there without saying good-bye. I was 6 years old. That night, I cried myself to sleep, holding on to my shoes, and waiting for my mother to come back and take me home. She finally returned … a year later. I then was forced to say goodbye to 34 'sisters and brothers' from the orphanage, who I would never see again, thereby taking away the connection and feeling of security I had reestablished, with this new found, family.

My soul was bruised by this cruel event and my heart scratched by the thorns of destiny. Back at my family's home, I clung to the roots of life, desperately searching for my family's acceptance which I would never find.

Later on, by learning to love my family unconditionally, the way they are and the way they're not, by giving them the love and acceptance they couldn't give me, I found peace in my heart.

Drawing strength from my own source of intuition by not depending upon anyone's opinion for my sense of identity or worth, I stayed true to myself, and followed my heart. At age sixteen, with my first paying job, I was ready to enter adulthood.

I left home and would never return to live with my family. With a great feeling of exhilaration for this new found freedom, the time had come to establish the limits and boundaries of my responsibilities to myself on an all-new level. By taking full charge of what was my duty and letting go of what was not, I began to understand first hand that discipline would be my ticket to greater opportunities and freedom in life. With great ambition, I took as big a step as possible—whenever possible, tackling one challenge at a time, sometimes juggling from one opportunity to the other, one bigger game to the next. I traveled from Paris to Madrid, London, to Los Angeles, with a sense of great expectations.

The country girl that I am met and conquered every challenge I undertook, whether it was family affairs, business affairs or affairs of the heart, I drew fresh inspiration from each lesson, and each new experience, with enduring passion. I must say I never did anything by halves. With an attitude of audacity, I took hold of my destiny—at times fierce and courageous yet remaining sensitive and vulnerable. I learned very quickly that no matter what we feel or know, no matter what our potential gifts or talents, only action can bring them to life. Those of us who think we understand concepts such as commitment, courage, and love, one day discover that we only truly know them when we act upon them. Only then, 'doing' become understanding.

Following the sometimes bumpy road of life I've found strength in always believing in a better tomorrow, as well as developing a sharp ability to observe order beneath chaos. By acquiring from each experience the wisdom to recognize blessings within adversity, and the self-honesty to perceive the cause behind calamity as well as having an awareness of divinity, the design, and purpose behind life's joys, and all of its obstacles.

By actively using whatever arises, embracing even the most painful circumstances, I dealt with my difficulties more effectively and began to see them as a form of spiritual training.

Having had to face many difficult situations, I can say that the excitement about life for me is that it's like music notes; no matter how bad the music, we can re-arrange the notes as we please and recreate new more pleasant sound. No matter the circumstances we have the Power to choose our directions and change as many times as we please.

I am convinced that it is not what has happened to me that matters most but rather how I choose to react to it. Like water flowing between rocks, I have had to reinvent myself several times. Learning new cultures, new languages, and new countries.

While redesigning my life, and starting over from scratch, and always maintaining my desire to be staunchly independent—flexibility and courage have prevailed.

The timing of my journey, as well as the discipline and faith I applied, was for me to choose. Trusting in the process of life, keeping a great sense of humor, and above all, remembering that it is never too late to experience the life I was meant to live. Life is full of good surprises for those who don't give up on themselves. Keeping in mind that no one else is responsible for my happiness, or for that same matter, my sadness.

Trusting the bigger picture, even during times when nothing seems to make sense and everything seems so wrong, my soul made no mistakes. 'It' watched over me, never left me, judged me, or lead me in the wrong direction. It has been my silent partner every step of the way, my connection to the higher power, the 'gate keeper' of the final picture of my life, the trusting voice and reassuring feeling that I have come into this world already knowing more then I know, more than I will read, hear, or study. Every experiences, challenges and lessons have all played an important role to who I am today. Who would have known, that so many blessings could emerge in the midst of such a chaotic start in life? Reflecting back on my achievements in becoming an internationally acclaimed Permanent makeup expert, featured on national TV and magazines, with 4 national recognitions along with an impressive clientele who are in the "Who's Who" list of Hollywood, living a life beyond my wildest dreams, knowing deep down inside my soul that whatever lies before me and what lies behind me are small matters compared to what lies within me.

What difficulty are you experiencing today? Look and see if you can see the Light hidden within it. What steps can you take to make it better? Can you see the bigger picture? We are created to be joyous and loved. We are more than capable of feeling good even when we feel bad. Live with great expectations and great things will happen. It is never too late to become what we might have been. Around the corner there may await a new road or a secret gate. There is a 'hero' in each of us. Speak to him and he will come forth.

When remembering the past journey, it seems as if so much has happened, yet when looking forward, it always seems as if the journey has just begun. As I continue on this voyage, to live a life of purpose, I cherish the path, honor the teachers, and humbly accept the lessons learned along the way. I maintain a feeling of gratitude for a life of blessings unfolding in the land of limitless abundance.

Do you ever look at the sky, the ocean, a hundred year old lady, or a newborn, in awe? Whenever I do, I am overwhelmed with a sense of humility and gratitude for life. These moments of awareness lift me up and give me great insights to live a purpose-driven life.

Look upwards today. Be in awe. Feel the immensity of life, know that you are a perfect part of it, and remember to make the most of every moment.

About the Author:

Dominique Bossavy's *passionate disposition, combined with her long list of award winning innovative techniques, has fueled her rise as an internationally acclaimed expert in the field of Permanent Makeup. Embraced by Hollywood's elite, her work often graces the red carpet. She is recognized as a National Treasure, by the American government, for her contribution to burn and cancer survivors. To learn more about Dominique's Permanent Makeup makeovers, visit* www.PermanentMakeupMD. com *and receive a free report* 10 Secrets To Perfect Permanent Makeup. *She can be reached via* info@PermanentMakeupMD.com *or* 310-772-8137.

CHAPTER 25

Forgiveness Isn't an Act,
It's a Process

Natacha Cann

Have you ever been fired? I have. On a Monday afternoon my boss called me into his office at 4:55 p.m. for a meeting. I thought I was being called in to finally discuss the outstanding evaluation he'd just completed on my work performance. Instead, he terminated my contract.

It became clear I was really terminated because I was only one of several employees who exercised my right to submit a rebuttal contesting the fact that my annual evaluation was two years late. Although unintended, my rebuttal naturally shed light on my boss's excessive mismanagement of his Department. He decided that instead of addressing my rebuttal, it would be best to fire a good employee.

Can you think of a few words to describe how I felt after being wrongfully terminated? I felt angry, betrayed and just outright flabbergasted that such a harsh verdict could be rendered without due process. I was under contract so I couldn't take legal action. Several attorneys confirmed that what he did was unethical but perfectly legal.

Since I had no legal recourse, I just wanted closure. I wanted to close this ugly chapter of my life and move on. But, how do you let go of the fact that you were wrongfully terminated? How do you let go of the anger? How do you deal with knowing that your boss was unethical but he gets to keep his job without consequence?

For me, it was not just a matter of *how* to let go, it was also a matter of *why* I needed to let go. I'd always wanted to become an entrepreneur and losing my job actually provided that opportunity. However, I knew I'd never be successful in life or business if I harbored bitter feelings about this incident and toward my boss. I didn't want this experience to consume my very essence! I needed a clear mind, body and spirit to undertake my new venture. Closure was not an option, it was a necessity, and the only way to get closure was to forgive, let go and move forward. So, that's exactly what I did.

Forgiving was *my secret* to creating the business and life of my dreams because it freed me of all emotional, physical and spiritual impediments, thereby allowing me to pursue my dreams without restraint. But the secret was not just in the *act of forgiving*—it was also in the *process of forgiving*. And that's the key—*forgiveness isn't an act, it's a process*. The *act* of forgiving involves pardoning someone for an offense, but the *process* of forgiving involves letting go of the anger, resentment and negative emotions that do not benefit us.

Experience has taught me that if you don't go through this process, there will be detrimental and lasting affects. As a life coach I specialize in empowering professionals to identify and overcome any emotional barriers that may prohibit them from fully pursuing their goals and succeeding. Clients have expressed how an unforgiving heart caused them to hold on to anger and resentment to the point where it affected their ability to succeed. In one case, a gentleman "literally lost one year of his profession" because he spent all of that time being bitter over losing his job, rather than focusing on his career.

I thank God that I was able to work through the process of forgiveness and I now guide others to do the same. If you desire to be successful in life or business and if an unforgiving heart is holding you back, there are four things that you must understand in order to work through the process.

First, Understand Whom Forgiveness Is For

Forgiveness is not for the other person's benefit, *it's for your benefit*. Yes, forgiving is something that you must do in order to free yourself from all emotional pain and bondage. When you truly accept this fact in your heart, you will come to the realization that forgiving is about what "you" must do and the person "you" must become in order to heal and move forward.

Second, Understand Why You Find It Difficult To Forgive and Change the Way You Think

There are two common reasons why people find it difficult to forgive:

1. You Think You're Letting Someone "Off the Hook".
This is especially the case if the person shows no remorse or doesn't apologize for his/her actions. You may feel as though you are just *giving something away* by forgiving and the person has not earned it. Forgiveness, however, is not about what you give away; it's about what you gain.

2. You Want To Change the Other Person.
Have you ever thought, "I can't forgive because he/she was just selfish, insincere, inconsiderate, judgmental, malicious or hurtful?" If so, you won't forgive because you want to change that person. Forgiveness is not about someone else changing to make you feel better. It's about pardoning someone for his or her transgressions notwithstanding whom or what he or she is. So, it's really about finding it in your heart to change yourself.

Third, Understand Who Suffers the Consequences

Since forgiving is for your benefit, you suffer the consequences when you don't forgive. Situations vary, but here are three common consequences:

1. You Live In the Past.
When you can't let go of the past, it's exactly where you remain. You relive and rehash the experience; you feel the same anger, bitterness and resentment. You waste valuable time and energy focused on why someone should pay for their actions when you could be focused on moving forward.

2. You Give Up the Power to Command Your Future.
You cannot command your future if you're living in the past. You must be an active participant in your life today so that you may affect what happens tomorrow. Your past will only equal your future if you allow it to. Letting go of your past means you are ready to live in the present and command your future.

3. You Impede Your Own Progress.
When you don't forgive, you give birth to undesirable characteristics that will prohibit you from reaching your full potential. These characteristics will cause you to be out of sync with your divine purpose and bitter emotions will control your actions. The wrong that has been done to you becomes your crutch, your excuse for why things just don't go right. You will continue to punish yourself and stand in the way of your own progress.

Fourth, Understand the Power of Forgiveness

Forgiveness is a choice you make so that you may empower yourself to attract all in life that is yours by divine right. Scripture teaches us that, "One reaps what he cultivates." So, whatever you cultivate will surely return to you. When you choose forgiveness, you chose to cultivate freedom, harmony, compassion, mercy, strength and wisdom. These are the principles that will guarantee your success and happiness.

THE GIFT OF WISDOM

Growing up, my mother always told me, "*Sometimes you've got to give up being right to make peace.*" Up until the very moment I was fired, and even shortly thereafter, I thought this meant that when someone has wronged you, even when you know you are right, just call a truce. In other words, just pardon that person for the offense so that you can make peace with them and move on. My interpretation of my mother's advice was based solely on the "act of forgiveness" and I think this is where most of us get it wrong. When you feel as though you are right, the other person is wrong, and you must forgive them just because it's the right thing to, you feel a sense of injustice.

When my mother said, "make peace," she was not referring to the simple *act of making peace with the other person.* She was referring to making peace with oneself. Once I came to this realization, I understood that forgiveness was for my benefit. From this perspective, I no longer felt a sense of injustice and I was ready to work through the process. Thereafter, I began to experience the true rewards of forgiveness. I was able to heal, let go and move forward. Today, I'm living my dream of being a successful entrepreneur and my life, as well as my business, has been enriched.

About the Author:

Natacha Cann *is a mentor, certified life coach and co-owner of* Essential Life Coaching. *She works with motivated professional women who want to overcome emotional barriers so that they may be more and achieve more in life. To obtain free resources and a free copy of her Special Report,* 4 Simple Secrets to Design and Live the Life You Desire, Today! *visit* www.NatachaCann.com

CHAPTER 26

The Most Amazing Mother's Day Gift, Ever!

Wendy I. Coad

My students call me an amazing teacher—an imparter of wisdom. I've been teaching for almost 30 years, but I never considered it work because I love to teach people what I know, so that they too can have a better life. Nothing could be better than the life I'm living.

Did I mention I only work part-time? I'm living the life of my dreams, working only two and a half weeks a month. The rest of the time I'm at the beach.

I can hardly express how fulfilling it is showing people how to help themselves and others. I can't wait to get to my classes because I know there will be an amazing group of people waiting for the information that I can share.

I know that their lives will be changed forever, just like mine was and just like yours can be.

And just when I thought this couldn't get any better I was soon to discover…

"The Most Amazing Mother's Day Gift, Ever!"

I was just home, visiting my Mom, Irene, on Mothers Day.

My mother has inspired me all my life. She would always tell me to follow my dreams. Even when my dreams led me to a career in art, with not much money to be earned, she supported my decisions and celebrated each little victory. She may not have shared my specific passion but she understood what it was like to be passionate and wished me a life full of experiences, happiness and knowledge.

And passionate she was, about life. When my sister decided to travel the world, Mom encouraged me, at age 19, to go with her. We traveled the globe for 2 years and she was happy to join us at various stops, even though we were roughing it all the way.

Her motto was *"live for today for tomorrow may never come"*.

My mother has survived cancer 4 times. That's right, 4 times. Each time a separate organ, each time an operation with chemotherapy and/ or radiation. All of this happened 30 years ago. Need I say more about the strength of this woman?

She started out as a farm girl, so poor she couldn't afford an education past high school. But someone saw the kindness and spark in her and they sponsored her training as a registered nurse. She did hospital nursing as well as private nursing. That was when nurses did everything: cook, clean and care for the invalid.

When she had her cancers, I think the nurse in her took over. She knew that she had to find a way to heal herself. A stay at an organic farm to learn how to change old habits is probably what allowed her to stay cancer free after the last bout. Medicine was different 30 years ago, the treatments were less refined and the surgeries left great craters and scars across her body, but still, she was alive.

Being alive was what she did best. She embraced life and encouraged me to do the same.

She and her sister also took classes in health and even a workshop in Reflexology. Just for interest though, she never did much else with it. My great uncle, however, had been a Reflexologist, practicing in the early 40's and 50's.

For those of you who might not know, Reflexology is a complementary health practice that has evolved through time to become one of the most effective and popular bodywork techniques offered today.

The principles of Reflexology conclude that by applying specific alternating pressure to areas of the feet and/or hands and ears, the whole body and all the organ systems can benefit. Through this technique, stress and tension can be greatly relieved and the body tends to feel renewed, strengthened, and returned to balance.

I thought I'd left the family traditions long behind. All the pharmacy (father), and medicine (mother), was something for others in the family to follow. I was going to be a great painter, painting people and figures.

It was an easy transition from artwork to bodywork and soon Reflexology became my passion. It never occurred to me that I had followed in my mothers footsteps until my husband pointed out what now seems so obvious.

"The first time I came to your apartment I saw a wall of Aromatherapy and all your books on Reflexology and bodywork. And, you don't think you've followed your family traditions?" he asked.

My whole life, I'd thought I had wanted and thought I'd gone in a completely different direction, but now I'm thrilled to be following my mothers lead. She taught me the power of kindness and strength and how to keep putting one foot in front of the other, no matter what the odds.

Today she's doing okay. Irene is well into her nineties and she has Alzheimer's.

Still, she's an amazing person and luckily, she's in a wonderful eldercare facility. Even though her recollection of me is dimming, we spend lots of wonderful time together. Sometimes we talk about the very distant past. At various times she considers me her mother, father, daughter, sister or a stranger.

One thing we can do together is Reflexology. And, since her hands are the easiest to reach, I often give her a soothing Hand Reflexology session.

Although the disease has decreased her responsiveness, as soon as I take her hand she turns towards me and smiles. Because of her cataracts, she can no longer see me but she can feel the warmth of my hands and the love in my touch. It's such a gift to be able to communicate with her in this way because so many avenues that I once took for granted have now been cut off.

We sit together, her hand in mine, and I slowly and gently do some Reflexology relaxation techniques. I use a little extra lotion and I'm careful not to pull the dorsal skin. Her skin is extremely thin and the vessels are very prominent. On the palm side, I scoop my fingertips in just a little bit. Her hands are often cold so I wrap my hand around each finger and give a gentle squeeze and never any heavy push or pull, but using only the lightest, most gentle touch. Sometimes she'll squeeze my hand back as if to say she's happy I'm here.

Holding each finger just as I described above can offer soothing balance to all the chakra elements as well. Not only that, half the meridians in the body begin or end on each finger tip. (We learn these techniques and so many more in my Advanced Hand Reflexology programs.)

Irene is usually sitting in a chair that's part-chair and part-bed. She no longer walks. There's not a lot of movement she can do. It's incredible that she has no specific organ issues. Still, all her systems are wearing down. It's action, movement, bending and straightening that keeps us mobile and our fluids flowing. Although she's not able to use these mechanics for system support and balance, I deeply trust that these Reflexology sessions help her organ systems as well as all the fluid tides.

I focus on the general session sequence and use just a fraction of the pressure, and one quarter of the normal time is used.

So, we sat together on Mother's Day, for those precious moments, in deep connection and communication without needing to say any words.

It was the best Mother's Day gift, ever, and it was one that Irene and Reflexology gave to me.

I will treasure it forever.

We live in a world where people are too often stressed and deprived of meaningful touch. To receive touch in a safe and compassionate way can have a powerful impact on anybody. If challenged by health or emotional issues, the soothing and relaxing touch that is Reflexology is one of the most powerful health supporting tools I know. If looking, always ask for a nationally certified Reflexologist.

Today, nothing could be better than the life I'm living. I think about Mom and how much love and caring she put into the world, and now I have an opportunity to do the same, each and every day. That's my passion, following my mothers lead, and helping to heal the world … one foot (or hand), at a time.

About the Author:

Wendy Coad *has a Masters of Fine Arts, a degree in Education, is a licensed Massage Therapist and currently a Director of the American Reflexology Certification Board (ARCB); a member of the National Certification Board for Therapeutic Massage and Bodywork (NCBTMB); the New York State Reflexology Association (NYSRA); and the Reflexology Association of America (RAA). For information call 800-875-1773, or for a free Report and E-newsletter on* Reflexology Secrets, Tips and Techniques *go to* www.ReflexologyProf.com

CHAPTER 27

How to Create a Masterpiece
Called Your Life:
The Power of Art and Aesthetics

Geoffrey H. Fullerton

DO YOU BELIEVE THERE IS ENOUGH BEAUTY IN THE WORLD? Contemporary artist Tomasz Rut didn't believe so. In fact recently at an art auctioneers' conference I attended, he was asked what was his greatest motivation to paint such impressive works of art. He said, "When I was young I decided that there wasn't enough beauty around and I wanted to contribute to beauty in the world."

Today with all that we see happening around the world and our communities—wars, drug abuse, and violence, to name but a few, it becomes difficult to know where the beauty is.

The concept of beauty has been around well before mankind happened upon this globe. Nature has it in abundance. The concept or idea is called aesthetics and mankind, definitely affected by it, had to create a way to emulate it. That emulation became known as art.

In my art enrichment program called "7 Insider Secrets to Collecting Art", I present the concept of collecting art to be as simple as "A.R.T." 'A' stands for Aesthetics, 'R' stands for Relative value in the marketplace and 'T' stands for Talent. This all relates quite well to collecting art, but how on earth does it relate to creating a masterpiece called your life?

Understanding the original meaning of the words art and artist will cause you to realize its necessity in most everyone's life. The oldest basic meaning of art circa 1225 is, 'skill as a result of learning or practice.' So an artist is one who is skilled as a result of learning or practicing. With that knowledge we can better understand what Mr. Picasso was saying and how you, as an artist, can make a masterpiece of your life with the use of "A.R.T."

"Every child is an artist. The problem is how to remain an artist once he grows up."

—Pablo Picasso

Aesthetic: 'A set of principles underlying and guiding the work of a particular artist or artistic movement.' E.g. *the Cubist aesthetic.* So, what is the [your name here] aesthetic?

Every successful person I've met has had certain principles that guide them. Aesthetics, (an idea of beauty), can be used in your everyday life. Aesthetics has to do with beauty and most importantly your concept of beauty. So, what's beautiful for you?

The surest way to develop your aesthetic is to take care of yourself. Just the basic practice of taking care of yourself physically, mentally and spiritually will definitely enhance your aesthetic. Here's how it could apply to you:

Your Physical Aesthetic

How you dress, groom and healthfully take care of yourself is a quick start on creating a masterpiece life. As well as looking and feeling good, you'll be cultivating *poise*, a characteristic that will be both envied and desired by most of the people you meet. This is a part of every great aesthetic example.

Your Mental Aesthetic

One of many ways to cultivate a supreme mental aesthetic is by adding culture to your life. Get into the arts, collect fine art, read good literature, travel and experience other cultures. Hands down this makes the mind more beautiful. Feeding the mind on the arts and other expressions of human intellectual achievement, regarded collectively, will assist in establishing your mental aesthetic.

Your Spiritual Aesthetic

A spiritual discipline for many of us forms the underlying and guiding principle in our lives. Given genuine attention and consistent daily practice, such discipline leads us to discover the deeper beauty in our lives. You'll probably find yourself taking more deliberate action in creating beauty in your life and in the lives others.

Imagine living your aesthetic on all three levels … physically, mentally and spiritually! You walk into a room and people feel the beauty, the aesthetic in your life. Many times they'll see it before you ever do. That's the creation called you: the Life Artist in action!

> *"At the age of six I wanted to be a cook. At seven I wanted to be Napoleon. And my ambition has been growing steadily ever since."*
> —Salvador Dali

Relative value in the market place. In the art world many people are asking the question: Is art an investment? The appreciation of a work of art is both desirable and important to many collectors. The real question is however, what will this work of art be valued at in the future?

How much are you valued currently? What will you be valued at in the future?

Creating your life as a masterpiece very much has to do with your relative value in the marketplace.

I'll never forget every first day of school between fourth and twelfth grade. It was during this period that I began learning the key to establishing my relative value in the marketplace. Standing in a very authoritative way, as he usually did, my dad congratulated us (my siblings and me) on heading into another year of school. He then, without a pause, stated that our mother and he needed to remind us of something very important.

Then he calmly said, "Now, remember you are black and you have to do 100% better than that white child sitting beside you." Now this may sound shocking to you, as it was to us, for we, at first, didn't have a clue of what he was talking about. By the time I entered Eighth grade I started to get it. I got it to the point where I had my Mom create a t-shirt for me in the colors of the Jamaican flag (my country of birth) that said, "Black is Beautiful". I wore that shirt around proudly (sporting an Afro hair style too, I might add.) I was obviously stating my own beauty or aesthetic. But it was later in life, high-school and then college, that I truly understood what my dad was impressing upon us—Succeed at 'knowing' you have worth and you will achieve! Value your own uniqueness because if you don't champion yourself, no one will. What a powerful realization to have and better yet, act upon! I began to understand my value, and in relation to those around me I continuously worked to increase my worth to myself and to others.

If you do that from a place that you establish and know your worth then you're in better control of your relative value in your marketplace.

"If people knew how hard I worked to get my mastery, it wouldn't seem so wonderful at all."

—Michelangelo

Talent. I'm curious. Would you like to own a work of art by Picasso, Rembrandt or Michelangelo? Why? Whenever I ask this question of my clients I get answers like "They're master artists" or "they're some of the greatest artists that have ever lived." It's no secret why most everyone on this planet has heard of these artists. Any major museum in the world has at least one of each of these artists' masterworks on their walls. One of the reasons for this is that they are artists of distinction and talent.

Talent, a natural aptitude or skill, is something that every artist has. The word that usually throws off most people is 'natural'. How many times have you said, "Oh, I'm not creative" or "I don't have any natural talent." Well, it's there. It just may need to be polished and shaped a bit in order to revealed.

Have you ever seen a rough diamond? It's unshaped, lack-luster and somewhat flat in its appearance. I hate to sound cliché, but we are all rough diamonds. (There I said it!) But here is what happens to a rough diamond. An artist comes along (you for example), takes that rough stone, shapes it, polishes it, and before you know it, this once rough stone with no 'natural' sparkle becomes a brilliant, valuable and invincible diamond! A masterpiece in the world of gemstones.

In order for most of us to be 'talented' we've got to study and practice our 'art'. I remember hearing the Jamaican saying: "Practice a yaad before yu go abroad". Translation: Practice at home before you go public (for those of you non-Jamaicans). That's how many people discover and develop their 'talent', just like Michelangelo, through plain and simple hard work.

> *"Life is not a support system for art. It's the other way around."*
> —Stephen King

The main thing is that if you truly feel there's not enough beauty in the world, then you can take responsibility for that by starting with yourself. Create more beauty in your universe. Believe me, it will catch on with those who are able and you're bound to start a renaissance.

The understanding of your personal aesthetic, your relative value in your marketplace and your talent will truly reinforce your position as the artist of your life. Once you feel this happening, you're on your way to being 'in power' and you are creating a masterpiece called your life. Now grab your brush, paint & canvas and create a masterpiece!

About the Author:

Art auctioneer and public speaker, **Geoffrey Fullerton***, "The Art Brotha" is the creator of the enrichment program "7 Insider Secrets to Collecting Art"™ and the TV show, "Got Art.TV". Combining 20 years in professional sales and 5 years as a principal auctioneer, Geoffrey provides a fun and workable system that assists his clients to easily understand aesthetics and acquire fine art. Contact him at* Geoffrey@art-brotha.com *or* www.art-brotha.com *for a free special report.*

CHAPTER 28

Inspiring the Amazon Within™

KYLE KING

One morning, I woke up from an incredible dream. I had gone to an event that night in Berkeley where the topic was the development of a Department of Peace at the cabinet level of the US government. The war in Iraq was fresh and I was not only upset but also scared. One of the speakers made a passionate call to women. She challenged us to step up and make the changes within our hearts that would effect change not only in our own lives, but also in the lives of all the people of the world. I felt like she looked directly at me when she said,

"Women are in the shadows and we must not remain there. We have the power to give life, and we are fierce when it comes to protecting our children. The victims of wars are the children—they lose their future, and consequently we lose ours!"

I left that auditorium feeling the amazing sense of "something's happening" but I didn't know what it was. That night I dreamt of an older woman, with long grey hair and bright blue eyes. She took my hands in hers and looked deeply into my eyes. Then she looked up at the sky and I followed her gaze. I saw an infinite group of women filling the atmosphere. They stared back at me with expectation and the old woman said to me:

"Inspire The Amazon Within"

In the morning I felt incredible, and knew she was naming something, but I didn't know what. I knew that the Amazons were women who stood up as warriors in an effort to subdue the rising tide of hierarchal tyranny (patriarchy), during the Bronze Age, some 5,000 years ago. I knew they were leaders, priestesses, warriors and queens and probably enacted the first resistance movement in human history. I also knew that they were an incredible archetype for my own life and for contemporary women. Without completely understanding what was happening, I trusted something was occurring that would transform my life.

When I was a very young woman, I had been drugged and raped by a "friend". A year after that, I suffered several brutal beatings from my boyfriend. Those events were catalyzing experiences which forced me to choose how I would behave in my life. Instead of hating *all* men, I became wary of most of them. Instead of becoming meek, I looked for imagery of women that were powerful and autonomous so I could model it.

For years I studied female cultures and artifacts dating as far back as 10,000 years ago. I found loads of imagery that satisfied my quest for honored and powerful females. I gave birth to 5 children at home, and nursed them continuously for 13 years. I started women's groups, and studied astrology to further empower myself and understand human behavior. What I didn't uncover, much less deal with, was my incredible sense of worthlessness.

I never really dealt with the abuses I suffered with the result being that I constantly settled for less than what I wanted. I was also unable to feel completely responsible for my life. I blamed society, men, and even my parents for the problems I kept experiencing. I had married a man I loved, but instead of standing up for what we had agreed to in our vows, I tolerated appalling incidents that occurred—thinking it would get better somehow. Our children and our love were the glue for us, but my marriage suffered from my lack of expression, and ultimately ended after 15 years. I ended it, and was branded as an adulteress (which I wasn't), but I felt such pain at the ruins of my life, I internalized and accepted that as well. I'd ripped apart my family, hurt my husband, neglected my children, lost many of my friends and most of the money I had.

I realized that I was completely powerless—not powerful at all. It didn't matter what I knew about strong women, as I just wasn't one.

As with all positive change, a turning point can be subtle. For me, it was gradual yet remarkable. Looking back, I believe that my commitment to my children was the key factor in my life. I knew that no one really listens to the words we say, but learns through the clarity of our example. Being a parent gives one a huge task in 'showing' them, and not 'telling' them how to live their lives. They inspired me to reach for more in myself all the time.

My daughters found me one day after the divorce, slumped on the floor and crying with despair. When I noticed them looking at me, I defiantly told them as I wiped the tears from my face:

"Please don't decide who I am because of where I am right now—watch me get up from this and *then* choose how to live your own lives!"

Months later, I was having a typical negative conversation with my kids' father, typical in that he was accusing me of being… "such a victim". I'd heard that from him for years, and for some reason it sunk in this time. As much as I didn't want to admit it, I couldn't deny that he had a point.

I started to consider how I was approaching my life. I realized that I did spend a great deal of time feeling sorry for myself. I kept focusing on what I didn't like, didn't want, couldn't accept… and consequently got much more of it.

I'd heard for years "you create your own reality" but I didn't know how I could have possibly created so much difficulty. Then I noticed a remarkable thread. If I was passionate about something, I got more of it … and I had remained *passionately committed to my pain*. I thought about how unfair life was (and lots of "unfair" things kept happening to me). I was worried about money (and consequently, never had enough of it). I was worried about my kids (and my oldest daughter became very sick). I was afraid of getting old (and I ended up injuring both my shoulder and my back). I couldn't escape the truth. I was creating my devastating circumstances with my commitment to feeling sorry for myself.

The deep pain of my life was creeping up on me, just like when my boyfriend chased me down the sidewalk and pounded me to the ground. The thought, "my life is so stupid" crossed my mind and I became totally enraged. I felt like my skin was too tight for my body. I was crying and pacing my bedroom, with my lover looking at me as if I'd lost my mind. I had always been so…sweet. The fierce woman buried inside me suddenly showed up.

I took out a loan, hired a coach, and got down to business. I let go of my victim perspective inch-by-inch, thought-by-thought, and within a year I started coaching others. My income increased considerably, my body began to heal, and my kids began to thrive. I became more respectful to men and I became emotionally richer and more defined.

After the dream, I had even more direction. I had a subject to study so I read everything I could; I scheduled a trip to Turkey (home of the Amazons), and toured most of the country to deepen my research. With my research, four principals of the Amazon stance emerged:

- An Amazon Knows What She Wants
- An Amazon Stands Her Ground
- An Amazon Replenishes Her Energy
- An Amazon Takes Responsibility For Herself

As I brought my ideas to my coaching clients, I was floored by what happened. The results were remarkable! Clients were getting promotions, finding lovers, getting pregnant, losing weight, making more money, getting off antidepressant drugs, recovering relationships… it was a coach's dream.

I created a course called, Inspiring The Amazon Within™ which was met with resounding excitement by all the participants. These women's lives were improving exponentially, just as mine had.

Several months ago I reflected over the past 5 years of my life and I had to smile. After years of feeling insignificant and worthless, I'd found the internal power I'd wanted all those years ago. I'd begun to light a fire in other women's hearts as well. I had been directed and inspired throughout my journey and my life expanded beyond my wildest dreams.

I own a beautiful home in California. I am wildly healthy and active. I have a thriving business I love. My children are astonishing people who are loving, persistent, expressive and dynamic. I've remained in a loving and passionate relationship with a man for a decade, who is equally determined and autonomous—who encourages my expression and honors our agreements to each other. Most of all I am happy. I respect myself, and I'm clear that I can offer tools that transform.

In becoming my own version of an Amazon, I see the value of the woman who is fierce *and* gentle at the same time. A woman unafraid to share her thoughts or establish her determination in any given situation. A woman willing to believe that she can create what she wants in her own life.

It is clear that I now teach what I most needed to learn. And although my work won't change the whole world, it can change one life at a time. It is enough.

About the Author:

Kyle King *lives in Santa Cruz California with her amazing partner Rob Miller, a professional rock climber and fitness expert and two of her 5 children. The other three are thriving in Hawaii and San Francisco. She trains and coaches people from all over the world and all walks of life, through her* Inspiring The Amazon Within™ *course and one on one coaching. To learn more about Kyle and her trainings, visit* www.inspiringtheamazonwithin.com *or call 831-818-3898.*

CHAPTER 29

Wise Beginnings: Building a Business (and a Life), on a Foundation of Spiritual Substance

Tom McAuliffe

So you want to build a successful business? Of all my years in business, as a builder; as a financial adviser; and now as a prosperity consciousness teacher, this is the best advice I can offer: Start wisely. Start with a clear vision of your desired outcome, and then work from a firm foundation. Build from the ground up, as castles built in the air are notoriously flimsy!

So what ground do you stand on? How do you relate to this world we live in? Are you safe here? Is this world a helping, healing place or a hostile place? And what do you believe to be the source of 'All That Is?' Do you limit yourself to the simple material reality as it presents itself, or are you open to a deeper appreciation of your own source? These beliefs not only influence your life but substantially control your destiny.

As a consciousness teacher I know we all carry internal programs, (or beliefs), of both abundance and lack. What is not well understood is that the lack programming is a conditioned or learned belief and can be unlearned, while the abundant, prosperous consciousness is the ground of your being, your innate natural goodness. You are innately, implicitly abundant, but we have allowed conditional reality, a world of lack and limitation, to have rule over us, or at least hold us back from all of our good.

The universe is a helpful, healing place in my experience, and it is conspiring to bring you to ultimate happiness, in the here and now! How do I know this? Through this simple extrapolation: Everyone makes the best decision they can at the moment they make it, with the information they have at hand. We all strive for happiness—no one really asks for unhappiness for themselves.

So if we all are like flowers leaning towards the sun and our ultimate goal is happiness, what does this tell us about the universe of which we are part? Just as an orange tree must grow oranges, and the rose bush roses, we are grown of a place that must express goodness, happiness and love. It is the nature of the Cosmos, and it is our nature. You and I are full expressions of the universe, and as such we can be no other way than happy, loving and good.

Unhappiness is a learned behavior, a conditioned reality, just as a life of lack and limitation is born of self limiting beliefs. If you believe you only deserve so much happiness, you will get only so much happiness. If you believe you are not worthy of more joy, you will only get so much joy. By letting go of self-limiting beliefs we open ourselves to our unlimited potential and the power of infinite possibilities, because this is our nature.

Just as the Cosmos expresses through us, we are also creative masters of our destiny. We are all artists, creating in every moment with the thoughts we are thinking, creating our perfect vision, as we see it, moment by moment. Napoleon Hill wrote in his masterpiece, *Think and Grow Rich*, "Thoughts are things, so choose yours wisely." James Allen wrote in *As a Man Thinketh*, "You cannot get figs from thistles," meaning if we want to grow greatness we can't be planting smallness. The thoughts and beliefs we hold about ourselves and the Cosmos create whatever we hold to be true.

There's an old Driver's Ed lesson that comes to my mind often: "Aim high when steering!" We affect our flow when we look to the high point of the curve. The road is always changing and so is our focus, but the focus of our sight must stay on the high point of the curve. If it does, then we reach our destination safely no matter what arises before us. If we align with what is our highest and best at all times, reminding ourselves of the unfolding goodness before us, we are assured of a happy landing.

Oftentimes this takes courage—courage in the face of suffering and pain and seemingly insurmountable obstacles. Many times the courage to press on when all seems lost is the difference between success and failure. Not only is it darkest before the dawn, it is often steepest before the summit.

So I urge you to have courage as you open to the new wonderful you. Courage is a characteristic of the heart and is from the Latin word for heart (cor). The heart is the most powerful muscle in your body and must be exercised. We exercise it by "having heart," or by "taking heart". We choose to remain open to that which is, as it is, and not let ourselves become closed off and small or resistant to life. Instead be expansive, see things clearly and act accordingly, with soulful presence and peaceful ease. This is courage.

When our courage falters it is helpful to have good friends around to support us. We read in the Bible, "For where two or three are gathered together in my name, there am I in the midst of them" (MATT 18:20.) This is the basis of Masterminding, a time honored technique of spiritual partnering.

One of the greatest proponents of Masterminding was Andrew Carnegie, who practiced it with the likes of Thomas Edison and Henry Ford. They used Masterminding to help each other find solutions to pressing problems. A good Mastermind group will do this and more.

It is ideal to Mastermind with an understanding of the nature of the benevolent universe, always unfolding in perfect harmony for us. Whatever your belief structures are about this, it certainly can't hurt to expect the best when you begin a Mastermind session.

A Mastermind group reflects back to its participants their divine truth. Suppose we can't quite believe something is true for us, like a new job that will satisfy our inner and outer needs. It really helps to have a friend who can believe it for us. There are many aspects of life that might seem out of my reach but I know when I am Masterminding with my prayer partners, I am engaging their power of belief to work for my good.

Your partner's belief in you supports your own belief in yourself and there are no obstacles that a committed heart can't overcome. The Mastermind practice works because we know we are powerful beyond belief—we just need to be reminded of it regularly.

There is one other practice that is a powerful tool for remembering our spiritual essence. It is the Practice of Wise Generosity.

In the prosperity consciousness class I teach, the students are asked to commit to gifting 10% of all of their income to the source of their spiritual sustenance for the duration of the class. If this sounds a lot like tithing to you, you are correct. I expect many of you reading this will have a visceral reaction to tithing. My own experience is probably the same as many of yours. When I heard about this class many years ago I resisted taking part as I was 'against tithing.' Somehow I ended up in the class one night and made the commitment to gift 10% of my income for the next 12 weeks. It took courage to stay in the class, and it took courage to make the weekly gift. And strange to say, it had a most positive effect on my spiritual and financial well being!

I believe Wise Generosity operates on a couple of levels—one spiritual and the other material. Materially, it focuses one on the realities of one's earning and spending patterns. If you are like a lot of people your income and expenses run pretty close together, sometimes right to the very last dime. Cutting out a gift to the source of your spiritual sustenance from a perceived tight budget might seem like foolish behavior. And yet what I've found is that I became more conscious of my spending patterns and more resolute in my budgeting because of the 10% gift. Before the end of my 12 week class I was earning more and saving more than I had ever before.

On a spiritual level, there is something about honoring your spiritual source and sustenance that empowers a deep trust. It is like saving a part of your harvest for the future, trusting that the source of your good will continue to provide. This is the wonder of wise gifting: as you align with source, consciously, cheerfully, and willingly, (but most certainly not dutifully), you are reminding yourself of your true worth and your true wellness. And from this mighty source all goodness flows.

It is my hope and prayer that these few simple practices will open you to the wonder and power of an all loving Cosmos and your place in it. May you live your life to its fullest potential and may you and all beings everywhere be happy.

About the Author:

Tom McAuliffe *is a financial planner and investment manager, using a values based approach which emphasizes the wise use of wealth. He also teaches classes at his spiritual community on the practical and spiritual matters of creating an abundant life. You can reach him at 800-963-8880 or* tom@WisdomOfGenerosity.com.

Visit www.WisdomOfGenerosity.com *to learn more about* Masterminding with Spirit, Wise Generosity, *and to sign up to receive a free prosperity meditation downloadable audio file.*

CHAPTER 30

It Will All Work Out in the End

KATRINA SAWA

Ever since high school when my parents asked me "What do you want to do when you grow up?" I would say, "I don't know…", when really inside I think I always knew I wanted to have my own business, I just never knew what it would be.

I think they were a little concerned when after five years of college, no internships, lots of sorority parties, over ten thousand dollars in debt, and only restaurant or retail jobs under my belt, and two years later I was still bartending at a local Mexican restaurant. Then I signed on with a door-to-door sales company….what must they have been thinking??

I know what I was thinking…."Something will come my way that I was destined to do. It will fall in my lap like everything else I want does but only when it's good and ready." I've always been that overly positive person everyone gets sick of hearing saying "it's going to be ok, it will work out."

It's true though, "everything does work out in the end" – this has become my motto.

So, on my path of career exploration (since I felt I needed to get a "real job"), at age 27, here I was, about to get married. My best friend recommended me for a job—my first corporate world experience. I finally got on a more professional and financially stable track. But, in those three years, I learned I didn't want to work 70+ hour work weeks, nor did I want to wear suits, nylons and pumps in 110+ degree heat!

So, I moved on to another corporate position but something more fun: advertising sales. I excelled and loved this job for two years, but worked 60+ hour work weeks and stressed a lot over deadlines. I'm aging by the second….and still married, trudging through the long hours which, of course, the hubby didn't like.

Then, I thought, "Okay, if I'm going to work that hard, then I want more money, less stress and a better title with opportunities to move up the corporate ladder." So, I took a job as a Marketing Director. But after strenuous corporate training, more stress, six years with no vacation at any of these corporate positions (not even a honeymoon!), and 50+ hour work weeks at this job, I lasted only six months before I blew.

Yes, I blew. My boss and my environment were both negative and unsupportive. So, I picked up and left.

During that last corporate job I decided to consult with a Business Coach to help me figure out what I really wanted to do with my life. After working with her for three months, I realized that what I really wanted to do was solve people's problems. She even helped me figure out what kind of problems I would solve. The experience with my Coach confirmed what I always knew in my heart—I needed to be an entrepreneur.

This was a very important step for me because #1—I never thought I needed "help"; #2 – I didn't want to pay for "help" that wasn't needed; and #3 – I was a coaching skeptic.

I jumped right in and started my own marketing consulting business on a shoestring budget and my bubbly personality. I'm not sure where I got the confidence or how I thought it would work out, but K. Sawa Marketing was born. Now I could work flexible hours, wear casual clothes and be responsible for myself. Had I not gone through the coaching step, there is no way I would be where I am today.

It's funny though, that when I started my business back in 2002, I had no idea if I could stay focused during the day or not. I was afraid I'd spend my days watching *Oprah* or shopping 'til I dropped. Nevertheless, once I started getting clients that needed my help, I was automatically busy working.

I should also mention that my support system was not great. My parents thought I was nuts, but they helped me financially replace my income for 6-9 months so my husband and I could live without the stress of bills piling up while I created my business. My husband, on the other hand, wasn't so supportive. Looking back on it, I know he was just scared about money, bills and "what if it didn't work out?" It was hard to keep up the belief in myself that "I knew I could and it would all work out in the end" but I did it, and I did it alone. What saved me was my networking.

I found that getting out networking and meeting new people as much as I could, made me happy. The people I met and whom many I consider family, made me feel appreciated and they believed in me and in my abilities. Those are the feelings and things I craved so deeply at this point in my life; feelings I did not get from those closest to me. This was the hardest struggle throughout my journey and it wasn't even something "in" my business at all.

My business model was outlined in my business plan, which I wrote up in a free class offered at the local Business Information Center. I found that the messages and marketing strategies I was using to market my business were very unique in my area. Plus, I had a knack for building relationships. I chose to combine these skills and turn them into services and products I now offer my clients – called my JumpStart Your Marketing Series. These strategies I used quadrupled my business within four years.

I have a unique ability to "talk" to my specific target market—entrepreneurs and independent or direct selling consultants, on their level, about what they needed most in their business—effective and inexpensive marketing. So, I quickly built hundreds of relationships and was busy all the time solving marketing problems. I couldn't have created a better job for myself if I tried.

But there lies the problem…..I had created a job for myself. I was back to the 70+ hour work weeks and my balance in life was off, yet again. In fact my marriage was suffering.

At this time, I was used to "doing it all" like most entrepreneurs. However, I realized how valuable my time was. If I was ever going to be really successful and wealthy, I needed to let go of those things I was doing that weren't directly making me money.

So, now as I approach the end of my fourth year in business and I'm one year divorced with my own house and bills, I'm finding the need for more personal growth. I managed to keep my business alive and prospering quite well through my divorce, which meant a move for the business, interruption in services and a transition in my whole entire living situation.

I've been working at it for almost nine months now, my balance in life that is, and I've managed to restructure my business in such a way that now I charge more, work less and make more money than before. I've outsourced as much as I can; with an attorney, financial planner, CPA, bookkeeper, data entry assistant, virtual assistant, company for website design and updates, internet shopping cart, personal fitness trainer, two insurance specialists, landscaper and soon to add a house-keeper to that list!

So now I see the sun on the beach, the Margarita in my hand and now….I want more! More free time, less work, more money, more, more, more than ever before!!!

So, herein lays the new challenge….how do I evolve from here? Why is life such a constantly changing palette of all kinds of colors that we have to paint into a pretty picture for ourselves? We don't get a color by numbers chart or graph to go by, just a paint brush and a bunch of paints with a clean canvas ready to go. It's hard to figure out what to paint but now that I know what I want to paint: Me on the beach with my second husband at our second or third home. Making over a million dollars in the year 2011 and working from the internet, phone and a little in person each year, plus giving back to my community in various ways – I'll always be networking!

So, how do I get there?

I choose to invest in "me", from here on out.

I now believe that I can be wealthy if I choose to be. I don't have to do it all myself and I can more effectively solve my target market's problems. Most importantly, I choose to only surround myself with positive, supportive people.

I'm actually on the verge of my biggest challenge now and I feel it's ok to step out into new waters, try new things, spend money on new ideas and learning, teach myself new tricks because I fully believe…."it will all work out in the end."

About the Author:

Katrina Sawa *works 1-on-1 with entrepreneurs and independent or direct selling consultants advising them on the most effective, least expensive ways from A-Z to market their businesses. Katrina specializes in marketing planning meetings which give her clients clarity, focus and direction saving many of them thousands of dollars and hours of time in misguided marketing actions.*

Get Katrina's Free Report on How to JumpStart Your Marketing *as well as her* Free Marketing Tips, *at* www.JumpStartYourMarketing.com

CHAPTER 31

Reinventing Yourself—Fast

Frances Strassman

It all started when I decided to stop being a chicken. Big changes come to me—actually they sort of arrive prepackaged—when I am doing "something else". You know what I mean.

I have been self-employed most of my life, but I've spent the last eleven years developing my business as a Professional Organizer, specializing in imaginative ways to successfully organize the chronically disorganized—people so disorganized that it affects their ability to function comfortably. The secret of my success was I invented novel systems for the unique problems of each client. My clients were happy. Life was safe and steady.

But, There Was A Hitch

I have been a risk-taker in many aspects of my life. But when it came to finances, life long money fears meant that I never invested enough into my business to expand out to the broad range of people who could benefit from my innovative solutions. I wanted to grow, to stretch myself, but found I was holding on to my money even tighter since 9/11.

Instead of looking at the bigger picture, I settled for a little tiny niche—the chronically disorganized—inside this new large diverse industry of organizing, which was growing rapidly. I didn't do any networking and I didn't expend cash for proper marketing. Instead, I just worked with referrals from my professional association and clients. It was a nice living, yet I continued to be bothered by the many people who were not being served by the standard ideas and tools of the organizing industry.

I knew that creative people tended to be disorganized. It was almost as if the more creative they were, the more chaotic their offices were. Home-office entrepreneurs, marketing people, writers, consultants, and artists tended to have a hard time staying sufficiently well organized to manage their business. Realtors and others in sales had cars filled with paper.

Some folks were not comfortable with agenda books, or computerized time-management systems. Highly intelligent, skilled, and educated people often found file cabinets unworkable, planning and prioritizing difficult, meetings unproductive, and the day exhausting. Ingenious approaches to organizing are critical if these creative types are to get on with their work, and make more money.

So, I subscribed to a newsletter about how to use the Internet for business development. I thought it might be good to get more of my organizing ideas out to people who had disorganization (nibbling at their success), undermining their success. But, as usual, I hesitated to invest. Then one day I saw an offer for something called "The Online Success Blueprint Workshop". "Frances," I told myself, "you should sign up."

Sounds Easy? Wrong.

It wasn't that simple. This workshop cost three thousand dollars—not the kind of money I was used to spending. Of course that would only be the beginning of the expenses. There would be transportation, four nights in a fine hotel, plus food. And there would be interesting and "needed" materials to buy.

The old 'chicken-out-about-money' response leaped out at me

again. Further, because I had underinvested in my business, the business was bringing in only a modest income. Putting out four thousand dollars, or more, for a few days, knowing bigger expenses would inevitably follow, would be a huge leap.

All of the "what-ifs" starting popping up in my head. Sure, I would get valuable training, but what if I couldn't sell what I created? And so on and so forth.

And where would I get the time to produce all these materials? This meant another business on top of my business. Where would I get the energy? I was hesitant. This decision called for a seismic shift in thinking.

A Virtual Cliff Ahead

Why was I even considering this as an option? With all these concerns bouncing around in my head, it felt to me that to set out onto this course was like throwing myself off a virtual cliff. Well, there were three reasons.

First, I understood that I had to step out of this perpetual position of over-caution when it comes to money.

Second, I was absolutely certain that a lot of creative people, working in a wide range of fields, were not getting the inventive solutions they needed to better organize their work. Inventive solutions were my specialty, honed over years of working with some really tough cases.

Third, this was a great opportunity to earn money in an interesting new way.

Well, you only live once. I jumped.

Jumping Lessons

If you've ever been in a big-risk position, whether buying your first house, getting the big job, or giving birth, you have experienced the state of "free-fall". This happens once you let go and just do it—whatever "it" may be. But once you find yourself in free fall, there's nothing more to be afraid of, because you're already doing the thing you feared. Plus then a million possibilities open up, forming a landing blanket like the ones firemen hold out.

Landing Lessons

Once I decided to risk that money, the ideas which had been germinating for years, began to sprout. My creativity started rising into brand new business concepts. I could see all the people I could link to, who could bring enrichment to my clients, and I could envision new computer tools.

This stepping forward onto a new path seems to light us up, setting free many dimensions, and sweeping aside many of the hesitations. Who ever thought so instant a transformation could come from my commitment to this risk? Commitment is such an interesting process.

I started meeting people who had launched new businesses with great success. People who had decided to advance their business development and were expanding their businesses online. My determination increased.

I made the decision to reinvent my business. I could produce a variety of materials for online sales: writing, CDs, tapes, classes, videos, joint ventures, interactive trainings. Maybe even workshops. And now I would do it for a bigger market.

Instead of my little niche, I would work for all the disorganized creative people who needed the encouragement, practical ideas, and support I was so good at designing for them.

Taking Off Again

Well, I arrived home on a Sunday night from that conference, slept-in until eleven the next morning, went to my desk before breakfast, and called the clients who I knew would not be well served by the new business. I gently explained I was going to phase them out, as I would no longer be the best one to meet their needs. I let them know who else could offer help, and told them about my new service.

I shed all my non-essential commitments, hired a virtual assistant, planned what I would pass along to her, and began streamlining the rest of my life. This was a new day, and a new way, so why waste time?

I took myself out to dinner that night; I was too scared and excited to stay at home. Between bites I designed my first big workshop. When I went home I began emailing people who I thought might want to attend. The more I worked the more ideas I got.

I'll tell you what is so interesting to me about all this. I should have figured this out years ago! Or, to explain this more accurately, it's something I have known for years but only as a theory, not as a felt reality.

There is a learning curve to everything, every single thing, including how to deal with fear.

Once you start stepping out and jumping off cliffs, you kind of get used to flying.

Don't think you have that kind of energy? Try reinventing yourself. You will experience energy like you haven't had in years, (a rocket going out into this amazing world). So get going. Get going now on that dream. Find some other people who are going the same way, form a circle of support, challenge your fears and then commit.

In retrospect, I think the key for me was learning to focus on what I have to give, on what I really want to share with others, instead of on what I want to sell. One of the things that has held me back was this intense dislike of the hype of marketing.

I felt that in using the Internet, I would not have to push my endeavors at agents, trying to sell them on accepting my work. That would feel exhausting. With the online approach the public can decide what is worthwhile. We each have unique knowledge we should not keep bottled up, because there are so many others wanting that knowledge.

This is a case of finding new ways to express the knowledge we have—knowledge that would benefit others—and then designing creative ways to make this knowledge available. This now felt to me to be an excellent investment. If we seek to provide the best possible information or product, it will always be needed.

About the Author:

Frances Strassman, *owner of* More Than Order, *is a consultant, coach and writer specializing in organizing techniques for creative personalities who "think outside the box". Frances lives in Berkeley, California. She can be reached through her Web site,* www.morethanorder.com. *A free report,* The Myths of Disorganization, *designed for the creative person who is "organizationally challenged" and a free newsletter with organizing information can be downloaded from this website.*

CHAPTER 32

A Wounded Healer
and the Gifts of Service

Jay Westbroook

Joy and success share a similar progressive path: making money is good; making money doing something you love is better; making money doing something you love and which is of service to others is best, and making money doing something you love and which is of service to others, and overcoming great adversity and obstacles to do so is divine!

This is the story of one who has been graced with tremendous adversity and obstacles—some visited from without and others created from within—and the tools used to transform suffering, to overcome obstacles, to choose integrity and authenticity, and to tread a path of service. For this author, the path of service to others has lead to the gifts of service, and to personal joy, national recognition, and multiple streams of income.

THE NIGHTMARE OF YESTERDAY

I was born into a poor, New York, theatrical, communist household, and had drilled into my head that money and those who possessed it were evil. Conversely, I was taught that poor people were good, simply because of their poverty and nothing more. This made future financial success near impossible.

I am also a survivor of ongoing physical violence throughout my childhood, and daily brutal, multi-perpetrator incest from age three to five, accompanied by severe beatings and being thrown into a pitch black closet to sleep. As a child, I was unable to distinguish between being evil and having evil visited upon me. Not surprisingly, I became angry and depressed, isolative, self-destructive, and blaming. Luckily, I discovered drugs and alcohol, which probably saved my life. However, they also made me stupid, and led to very poor decisions—decisions which put me behind bars in the state prison system, with double "five to life" sentences. In that setting, being young, cute, slim, and not gang-affiliated, I endured multiple gang-rapes throughout my incarceration.

Upon release, I was determined to not return to prison, but found myself uneducated, without skills or self-esteem. I was also hopeless, bitter, blaming, resentful, broken emotionally, spiritually, physically, and financially, Godless, filled with self-hate, fear, and entitlement, jealous of those with money or joy, and fantasizing success while continuing to believe that people with money were bad. I was no longer in a 6' by 8' cell; I had "graduated" to a self-imposed prison of bitterness, hopelessness, envy, fantasy, and fear. While this was not a formula for happiness, service, or wealth, it was a great place from which to start. I had no plans, little to lose, and a willingness to take direction. Wounded and suffering, I was unaware of how that suffering could become a vehicle to awaken compassion in me, for me, and for others.

Living the Dream Today

That compassion allowed me to become a Wounded Healer, working with dying patients and grieving families. Two years at community college were followed by attendance at USC on full scholarship, earning a Bachelor's and Master's degree, a certificate in counseling, and licensure as a Registered Nurse. After years as a hospice nurse, I had the opportunity to develop and serve as Clinical Director of the first Palliative Care & Bereavement Service in a community hospital in California. In that role, (which I continue to occupy), I have won multiple national and regional awards, and more importantly, have been of service to thousands of patients and families as they approach the end-of-life.

My life has expanded from both a figurative and literal prison of bondage and hopelessness, to one of service that has carried me to Harvard Medical School (as 2005 Faculty Scholar), to Capitol Hill (for a national award), to Nurse of the Year, and even back to prison to teach "Being With Dying" to the inmate volunteers of the prison hospice!

I have unwaveringly, and simply, been of service to the dying and grieving—the work I love—and that has opened the doors of infopreneurship. While continuing my clinical responsibilities, I have created *Compassionate Journey, A*n End-of-Life Education and Consulting Service. *Compassionate Journey* has empowered me to share with others my heart and my expertise. It has also created multiple streams of income through publications, public speaking that has evolved to the keynote level, consulting, training, web-based information products, and even expert witness work.

My life is graced. I have a loving long-term marriage, am healthy, own a Southern California home with a pool and guesthouse, and love my two adult Coonhounds (Willow and Wyatt), and two Coonhound puppies (Charlotte and Smokey). I live in the moment, walk with faith, do the work that I love, earn an excellent living, and am comfortable in my skin and at peace. While my work is becoming more and more infopreneurial, I will not abandon the clinical component of my work, for it provides the opportunity to be of service to the dying and grieving, and reminds me to walk with a soft belly, an open heart, a posture of exploration, and a certainty that the place where life and death meet is filled with God.

TOOLS TO TRANSFORM NIGHTMARE TO DREAM:

Okay, so here's where the "rubber meets the road." These are the keys to how my life changed from nightmare to dream, from limited to limitless, from struggle to ease, and from lack to abundance. I had a great place from which to start—I had been beaten into a state of willingness and humility by my misery and poverty. I was out of plans, had little to lose, and a willingness to take direction. I stumbled upon a fellowship of people who seemed happy and successful, but assured me they had been neither in their individual pasts. They were willing to share, for fun and for free, that which had facilitated their change. I surrounded myself with people who had what I wanted, even when my lack made me uncomfortable, and I remained teachable.

They comforted that part of me that was disturbed by telling me that what had happened to me as a child was not my fault. They disturbed that part of me that was comfortable by telling me that what I chose to do with those experiences was entirely my responsibility, and that neither blame nor self-pity would lead to change. I got to accept responsibility for my life.

One new friend, Francine Ward (www.EsteemableActs.com) suggested that if I wanted to develop self-esteem, I needed to perform esteemable acts. As I commenced to do so, not only did my esteem grow, but also I found expanses of time where I actually thought only of others, and not about myself. Another suggested that if I left my fantasies at the door, that all my dreams could come true, and that's exactly what happened. Initially, I didn't even know there was a difference between fantasies and dreams; today, I live in the difference.

I remember coming to realize that feelings were not chosen. When feelings come, they just come, and telling myself or someone else to simply not be sad, scared, angry, or guilty is silly and meaningless. There is no way to choose or stop my feelings; what I get to choose is my behavioral response to them. In the face of fear,

I can choose cowardice or courage; I choose courage. In the face of hopelessness, I can choose giving up or perseverance; I choose perseverance. In the face of loneliness, I can choose isolation or reaching out; I choose reaching out. When I commenced taking contrary action—choosing the scarier or more difficult behavior, the behavior of greater integrity and authenticity, both my personal and professional life blossomed.

Professionally, I was told: 1) "you get more water from a 500-foot well than from 50 10-foot wells," and 2) "go through the doors that are open." Now those may seem obvious to you, but to me they were revolutionary. I had always jumped from one venture to another, and/or repeatedly banged against a closed door while completely ignoring the open one next to it. As I focused solely on the constellation of issues surrounding end-of-life (pain management, symptom control, grief counseling, emotional and spiritual support, and empowered decision-making), I developed tremendous and valued experience and expertise. In turn, more doors opened to opportunities to be of service and to provide information to larger and larger audiences.

Finally, I learned that we see what we look for and hear what we listen for. When I look for problems, that's all I see; when I look for solutions, I am sure to find them. When I look for how selfish others are, that's all I see; when I look for supportive mentors, that's all I find. Today I choose to look for and see how blessed my life is. I get to joyously do the difficult work of being of service to the dying and the grieving. I am honored to be allowed this privilege, and excited to entrepreneurially make available my expertise, and live my life with *Power and Soul.* These are the *gifts of service.*

About the Author:

Jay Westbrook *is an award-winning clinician, an info-preneur, and a nationally recognized expert on End-of-Life issues, including pain management and grief.* *He is Clinical Director of a hospital Palliative Care Service and Clinical Director of his own company,* Compassionate Journey: An End-of-Life Education & Consulting Service. *Westbrook is an entertaining and inspiring speaker who presents powerfully on the transformative aspects of suffering and on using suffering to awaken compassion. Contact information: 818-773-3700 or* www.CompassionateJourney.com

CHAPTER 33

Becoming One with Yourself

JOAN MARIE WHELAN

My wish for you in life is to have all that you want for yourself. How does that wish feel for you? For me it makes me feel happy and excited, even relieved knowing that someone is wishing good for me.

In order to bring to you your hearts desires in life, one must feel your desires inside of yourself. If one piece of you is saying positive affirmations to yourself and others and then the other part of you is feeling insecure, less than or has a negative chip, how can you create your desires?

I believe it is also vital for you to be in truth with yourself, your emotions and feelings. If you are having a bad day or are mad at someone you should not lie to yourself. Feel for a moment where you are. The key is not to stay focused on that emotion but to ask yourself "Is there an opportunity for me right now to learn something from these emotions?" Ask yourself this valuable question when you are in a state you wish to release from your body. This is the only way to begin the steps of aligning your body and your Soul to create power within yourself.

A major ingredient for you to achieve this alignment is to determine who you truly are. Know at any time you can add or delete to your value list of who you wish to be. When I ask you who you are, what I'm referring to is your personality and characteristics. What are your values? Are you a powerful individual full of courage and strength? Are you tender and have compassion? How do you wish to treat others? Do you love and respect yourself? How do you wish others to talk about you?

My wish for you is to tell me who you are and what it is you specifically wish to experience everyday in life. This way we both know who is in the driver's seat and who is setting the course for your journey.

There is another key ingredient needed to achieve a value-filled life and believe it or not, it exists within you. It is located within your lower stomach and back area and it is called the solar plexus. When you begin to understand this concept and accept it as your own, you will discover and begin to feel rays of light shining within you.

Within our solar plexus is a potentially powerful force which I call the sunlight. That's right! The sunlight actually lives within you. The rays are shining in and through your whole body. This is your life force. How you maintain your light internally is exactly how your life will continually play out. Are you vibrating to a high frequency or a low frequency? You decide!

You control the magic wand! You can tell by where you are at emotionally in life by what you are focusing on with your thoughts all day long—things and ideas you wish to have or what you do not have or want.

Everyone in life has lessons to learn—that is why we are here. Check in with your inner feelings and emotions daily. What seems to be a trigger point for you? Do you like 'you'? Are you comfortable spending time with you and for the moment only paying attention to giving and receiving kindness, tenderness and joy to yourself? Learn to nurture yourself by listening to your body and soul and heeding their messages.

People do not realize in life that it is not selfish to allow yourself to be internally filled. As your light inside is nurtured, the light vibration flows out and automatically vibrates to those around you. Imagine when you are feeling whole and complete internally, the energy vibration can become contagious to assist those around you to also have the opportunity to re-create these same feelings inside themselves.

What are you looking for out of life? Do you have wishes to succeed at a greater level or know unconditional love in this lifetime, or even to know what it means to be completely in the moment of 'right now' feeling great peace and joy? It is important for you to allow the light within you to shine bright in order to allow yourself to be one with who you are.

Here are several tools to assist your light to shine bright.

1. You can not hide anymore.
What this means is you must accept your greatness. Realize you came here for a purpose. What is this for you? For me personally, I needed to accept all of me and feel comfortable with who I am.

2. You must ask everyday to have strength and courage.
Life takes courage, risk and perseverance. In order to fulfill your destiny you must prepare and realize inward strength through love.

3. You must fall in love with all of you.
If you do not, than who will? You pulsate to a specific vibration. What you feel about yourself internally reflects your external process.

4. You must like yourself.
Allow yourself to have moments of being fun and silly. Always allow room for play.

5. Know that life is full of opportunities at every moment. Even when something does not go your way.

6. In the mist of your greatest sorrow, moments of rejection or when you are experiencing pain, you must always have your heart open to receive a blessing.

In order for your life to flow like a river, you must allow yourself to release feelings that are not serving you. In life many of us are taught criticism, the word "No, you can not do that or have this." All of this programming must be released. The more you release what no longer serves you, the more the light within you can shine bright.

This is a process and you must be kind and gentle with yourself. It is very important to really breathe in from your core where your light lives and as you exhale, give yourself permission to let go of old stories and thought patterns.

I always encourage people to allow time for quiet contemplation. In fact, I have several meditation CD's that have produced phenomenal results by assisting people to deal with (and heal), various situations in their lives. I would like to share a very powerful process with you. The first couple of times this may require sitting quietly and calmly. You may wish to put one hand over your heart and the other resting on your lower stomach. Allow yourself to begin to feel and see the sunlight that lives within you. Feel yourself sitting in the warmth of the sun and focus your attention on receiving the warmth flowing in and through you. Say to yourself, "this belongs to me." How does that feel to you? That peace, warmth and unconditional love actually do belong to you!

As you are being in the sunlight, begin to feel the rays melt down in and through your legs, flowing down through your feet into the earth. Allow the mother earth to be your support team—a part of your foundation. Next allow the rays of the sunlight to rise up in and through you towards the heavens. Inside you is pure sunlight. Right now being in the light, choose what it is you wish to receive in life and allow it to flow in and through your sunlight. Focus on this for a few minutes. Now allow yourself to bring up a time when someone or something made you feel a certain way, such as inferior. Allow this scene to come forward, feel what the feeling was at that age and ask yourself where in this moment lies an opportunity for you to grow and heal. As you begin to see your new awareness on the situation, take deep breaths, blow out these inferior feelings and let the sunlight melt them away. As this is happening, focus on the feelings you wish to feel and the daily life you wish to experience.

You can do this process anywhere and at any time. To be powerful does take a lot of energy and momentum. However, once you are in the flow, it can and will always be there for you, just waiting for you to tap into its magic. Your 'soul' is the little girl or the little boy within you that always knows "yes" and realizes that the burning desire in you can be accomplished. Your job is to give yourself permission to be in alignment with your soul and accept yourself as a powerful and beautiful person.

About the Author:

Joan Marie Whelan, *is an internationally renowned Medium, Medical Intuitive, Master Neurolinguistic Practioner, and expert of Past/Present Life Regression. Joan Marie appears regularly on many National radio and television programs, as well as providing seminars and products to help resolve problems her clients encounter. For more information on* How to Become One with Yourself *and receive her free newsletter containing valuable tips and tools plus added bonuses with her products, visit* www.joanmariewhelan.com.

PART IV

From Surviving
to
Thriving

CHAPTER 34

From Victim to Victor:
How One Woman Overcame a
Seemingly Career-Ending Crisis
and You Can Too

WINNIE ANDERSON, SPHR, CEIP, CPBS

March 7, 1999, was one of those glorious late winter days that hints at the beautiful spring to come.

That morning after church, I tossed my gym bag on the seat beside me, got in the car, and backed out of my driveway. The next thing I knew, everything was completely black and all I heard was this strange noise close to my ear. I asked what was happening and a man's disembodied voice told me he was cutting my jacket to get me out of the car. "Well stop it," I said; "It's my favorite." Then I passed out.

I had been in an accident so bad that when the EMT's arrived on the scene they cancelled the helicopter that had been ordered to take me to the regional trauma center. One look was all they needed to decide the driver couldn't have survived.

But I did.

Being the driven, obsessive professional I was, my first words to my husband while I was lying in my hospital bed were "You've got to call me out from work." That's right. I could have died but I was worried about my job.

I spent a week in the hospital, another week recuperating at home, and then went back to work as if the accident had been a minor inconvenience. It was when I returned to work that I discovered how badly I had been hurt.

I had been left with double vision so pronounced that anyone I talked to would look over their shoulder to see what I was looking at behind them. I had short and long term memory problems so severe I would frequently repeat what I had said only moments before and I couldn't remember my wedding or honeymoon (although I did remember my husband and that I was married.) I had impulse and emotion control issues that would cause me to burst into tears over the slightest hurt or become furious at the tiniest injustice. I had a host of problems in the area of what's referred to as "executive functioning", which made it nearly impossible to perform my job as director of human resources for the local chapter of a national nonprofit.

Juggling multiple tasks had been such a part of my life before the accident I never gave it a second thought. Now the slightest interruption would cause me to forget what I was doing—even as I was in the process of doing it. I found myself sitting in front of my computer, hearing in my head the words of the email I wanted to compose, but my fingers refused to type them.

It was time to face facts and admit what had happened: I had permanent brain damage. Before the accident I had completed my Masters degree in the top 10% of the entire graduating class. Now I couldn't remember how to tie my shoes or perform basic math.

I realized I had to quit work to give full attention to my recovery. The process would prove to be long, frustrating, and extremely humbling.

Therapy became my full time job, and I was at doctor appointments most days of the week. I had cognitive retraining a few times a week with a top occupational therapist in order to re-learn how to learn and to develop thinking strategies to deal with my limitations. I saw a physical therapist to learn to deal with balance problems created by my double vision. I met with a psychologist to learn how to control my emotions and deal with the aftermath of the accident.

It was the cognitive retraining that was the most frustrating. The American Occupational Therapy Association defines it as "…treatment that helps individuals achieve independence in all facets of their lives." I define it as "torture."

I sat for 60 to 90 minutes in front of a computer playing various "games." They call them that because if they called them what they really are—"Blows to your self-esteem"—no one would show up and the doctor wouldn't get paid.

Each game was more frustrating than the last. One was similar to many of the video games kids play. It starts in a room with several doors and there's a monster behind one of the doors. If you open a door and find the monster, you're supposed to open another door to exit the room. The hard part is remembering where the monster is so you don't open that same door again. Each time you move through a door, you go to a different level and it gets more challenging. It took me weeks just to progress to the second level.

After tormenting me with that for 15 or 20 minutes, my therapist would change the game and I would do something even more difficult. Like basic math. And I mean adding two single digit numbers together basic. I'd sit there looking at the problem, knowing the answer should come instantly to me, but feeling frustrated and humiliated because I couldn't come up with the answer. Countless times I'd pretend I had to go to the bathroom, just so I could shut the door and cry. I would be 37 in a few months and basic math reduced me to tears.

I hated those sessions; but what I hated even more was recalling the ease with which I had once been able to perform such simple tasks. Since my long term memory was pretty much intact I was haunted by the memories of what I used to be. It was difficult to resist comparing the former me to the new me.

I often wondered why I survived the accident at all. I've always believed that everything happens for a reason, that there's a positive somewhere —a lesson to be learned in every situation or experience. I was determined to figure out the lesson in this; and I began talking to God, reading the Bible, and begging Him to help me understand.

It took a long time, but eventually I came to see the accident as an amazing gift. It had been bad enough to knock me off the high speed treadmill I was on and prevent me from ever getting back on it. It humbled me by showing me how prideful I was of my abilities. It helped me rediscover what's really important. It made me a better person.

Many people, including my doctors, are amazed at how far I've come and my ability to hold off the depression that often sets in when someone experiences this kind of trauma. Here's my advice for dealing with what seems like a mountain that's too hard to climb:

HAVE FAITH

I knew there was a reason this had happened to me and I had to figure out what it was. I didn't pull any punches with God. I let Him know how frustrated I was. I don't believe you shouldn't ask God "why." Ask Him. He'll help you figure it out if you remain open to the lessons to be learned.

STOP TALKING NEGATIVELY TO YOURSELF

We talk to ourselves all day long. We stub our toe and say "I'm such a jerk." Stop it. We should always speak positively to ourselves and it's most important when we're struggling with a challenge. Once I was able to focus on all that I could still do and all that I still had, I started to make greater strides in my therapy. I don't know where this quote originated, but I believe it:

Watch your thoughts, for they become words.
Watch your words, for they become actions.
Watch your actions, for they become habits.

Watch your habits, for they become character.
Watch your character, for it becomes your destiny.

Push yourself

Do a little more every day. Just as lifting weights makes you stronger, challenging yourself in other ways will do the same. When my physical therapist told me to lift a weight 10 to 15 times, I always did 15. The computer games may have made me cry, but I always composed myself and went right back to them. Don't ever give up. You shortchange yourself if you do.

Stay focused on what you want

I was determined to get well. Know what you want and keep moving forward.

Don't compare yourself to others

While it certainly helps to realize there are plenty of others worse off than you, never compare your performance to others. Only compare yourself to you.

Get help if you need it

It's not that your friends and family aren't interested in or concerned about how you're doing. They really want you to get past your challenge, but there's only so much they can hear about it. They have their own problems. Hire a therapist. Get a coach. Pay a professional to be your sounding board. Then, when your family and friends ask how you're doing, you can honestly and proudly say "Just fine thanks. How 'bout you?"

About the Author:

A brand strategist with award winning Abiah Designs, **Winnie Anderson** *coaches leaders to implement brand building strategies for their small to mid-sized businesses. Get free tips and learn how to stand out from the competition. Sign up for their bi-monthly brand building newsletter at* www.abiahdesigns.com. *Winnie's own newsletter helps business leaders create lives in sync with their values. Get a free chapter of her latest book when you sign up at* www.bloominfaith.com.

CHAPTER 35

Secrets of Health, Self and Wealth Discovery

BARBARA ANN BLAKE, HHC, AADP

For many years, I was a sugar addict who only ate 100% processed foods while on the run, along with stressful career, relationships, little to no exercise unless you count running through the airport ala the Hertz commercial or the occasional dance class and not being in touch with who I was what I wanted or needed. I call this living behind a beautiful façade that is eroding internally. I had reached a point where I didn't even feel the stress that had overtaken my body and life.

My list of health ailments was growing: high homocysteine levels, 30 excess pounds, feminine issues, and severe pain up and down only the right side of my body along with fever. I was unable to physically move, think or process information. My mom moved in to help take care of me. This wasn't the first time I had been plagued by a dramatic health issue. I had overcome past health challenges and persevered with my life. Looking back now, I never really addressed the causes of those illnesses and probably because of that, I was stopped in my tracks now. The conventional medical community didn't have any clear diagnosis for me. One of my possible diagnoses even showed up in a TV episode of *House*, yet confirmation remained elusive. A diagnosis is only a label after all. What caused the condition is much more important. Strong resilient bodies, minds and souls are the result of optimal nutritional intake and lifestyle for your individual body ecology. When you are maintained and taken care of optimally, outside environmental factors are less invasive. The body can take many years of nutritional and/or lifestyle abuse or just a few depending on your own individual ecology. Amazingly we are taught how to read, write, perform arithmetic and even operate a car or VCR, but we learn via life experience how to operate our body, mind and soul. Finally I recognized the importance of outside influences and factors that contribute to my health like stress levels, nourishment consumption, relationship strengths, physical exercise, career happiness, including the spirituality of who I am.

So Secret 1 is learning how to optimally operate your individual body, mind and soul

Learning how to operate your body mind and soul isn't an easy task by all means. 'Reach out and touch someone' was the tag line of one of the telecom companies I worked for, so I put it to use. I personally was clueless so I asked everyone I encountered what else I could be doing to recover my health. This line of questioning led and attracted the right mentors and alternative treatments into my life. I took my health into my own hands and went outside of the conventional medical establishments. My persistent asking and power of attraction led to a kinesiologist, acupuncturist, Chinese herbalist, body stress release practitioner and last but not least, a holistic health counselor. Each of these areas contributed significantly to my healing.

Secret 2 is you don't need to do it alone—ask for help

To this day I continue to ask what else I could be doing to improve my life and put my intentions out into the universe for them to be fulfilled. I personally sought out and worked with individuals and groups that supported my highest good. I eliminated/cut out what wasn't working in my life. I learnt in chemistry that mixing the same quantity of specific chemicals would always create the same result. It took years to realize that doing the same thing in life over and over also produces the same result. I tried doing everything opposite to what I would normally do. For example, I intentionally took the stairs instead of the elevator, and deliberately rose from the opposite side of the bed. Just by consciously making different choices I changed and so did everything around me—for the better.

Secret 3 is stop doing the same thing repeatedly and expecting a different result

Next, I overcame the conditioning of the outside environment that influenced my life and the decisions I make. I had been told I needed to work hard to succeed, i.e. get a good job and I'd be set for life. I had a very successful work life, made plenty of money, invested wisely and could purchase just about anything I wanted or desired. What I didn't have was the time to enjoy any of my possessions, relationships, or even exercise. The 'things' I gathered were just that—status and symbols to label my wealth and success. I wanted to please everyone and in the end I was the one who was never pleased. Basically, no one can live up to the expectations of everyone else or even yourself. Say hush to your inner critic. Most conditioning is fallacy so leave them all behind in the land of fairy tales.

SECRET 4 IS OVERCOMING THE CONDITIONING OF YOUR ENVIRONMENT AND INNER CRITIC

When I was living to please everyone else I felt the world just 'happens' to us and we have no control. I blamed what wasn't going right in my life on everything and everyone other than me. I realized what I did have control over was how I reacted to everything that happens in my life. I have the power to decide how I am going to react.

SECRET 5 IS EMBRACE THE POWER OF CHOICE

When I didn't make a choice and allowed someone to make that choice for me, I relinquished control of my life. Take back control of your life with the power of decision and choice. Just this one secret can revolutionize your life.

What you live, breathe and experience is up to you. Sickness was my signal to get back to self. It was a warning sign that I was out of balance. I took phenomenal self-improvement courses in NYC that put me on the right self-path by focusing on the power of right now and creating strategy and tactics for my life and relationship with myself.

SECRET 6 IS REALIZING THE POWER YOU HAVE WITHIN YOURSELF TO CO-CREATE YOUR LIFE

I began to incorporate universal laws into my day-to-day living and mapped out visually my wants, needs and desires. I left the person that I was behind and I focused on what I desired to become. We have all heard the saying what you focus on grows but what you ignore wilts. Well, now I focus only on my desires that support my highest good. I found that when I focus on what is best for me I have the energy and desire to get what ever I want done.

Secret 7 is stop putting everything and everyone ahead of your self

As a frequent business flyer I've heard always to place my mask on first than take care of others but never applied it to my daily life. Once I started to place my needs wants and desires first my life began to unfold. I was transitioned by what I believe the mind can achieve. I went back to school to learn how to operate my body, mind and soul. I was able to renovate my food intake and lifestyle, rebuilding my foundation and creating a maintainable wellness level. Through the combination of the schooling and the alternative treatments, I regained my health and along the way I discovered who I am, what I can become and how to go about it. I am grateful for all the prosperity and abundance that I have in my life even such things like water, air, housing, and health I used to take for granted.

Secret 8 is practice gratitude

I can live my life learning more about my health and self and make a living out of helping others on their quest to personal wellness. My well-being business and life is connecting people to their 'gut' both literally for nutritional consumption and figuratively for lifestyle adjustments in exercise, relationships, career and self.

In summary, I stopped doing the same things repeatedly expecting different results. I asked for help and figured out who would support, guide and assist me. I created a core group of dependable people to help my health, self and wealth grow and prosper. I continue to ask what else I could do to improve my life. I don't accept others guidance, statements and advice blindly. I make educated choices. I figured out how to work my own body ecology from the both the nutritional and lifestyle perspective. I am grateful for the abundance and prosperity I have every day. Continually I take care of myself and co-create the life I desire. And last but not least, I realize the world around us is not static, so be in tune so that adjustments can be made to keep us on the path of health, self and wealth. Make feeling good your number one priority everyday by applying these secrets to your life.

About the Author:

Barbara Ann Blake *is a Board Certified Holistic Health Counselor accredited by the American Association of Drugless Practioners specializing in empowering the individual to discover the relationship between eating, feeling, and living well. She founded* Blake Wellness, *a private practice in Manhattan, and regularly conducts health supportive cooking classes, lectures, workshops and counsels individuals in person and by telephone. Visit* www.blakewellness.com *to sign up for a free ezine on wellness topics or call 212-799-5580.*

CHAPTER 36

Self-catraz —
Escaping Your Personal Prison

Diane L. Broos

The Poem: "Self-Catraz" —
Your Personal Prison

I am reduced to a number
My home is made of stone and steel
I stand alone in my misery
Alone
My heart aches
Alone
No choices to make

Afraid
Of what might be
Afraid
What will happen to me?
Dreams vanquished

Plans undone
My hearts song
Left unsung
Prison
What it's done to me

—Diane L. Broos

Do you feel as though you are dying on the vine of life? Let me encourage you; it's never too late! Don't spend another day in 'Self-catraz' being constrained from living the life of your dreams. Act today: think different, do different and be different.

Has the key to my cell been thrown away? Is it too late for me?

Not many of us have been incarcerated in a formal prison. Yet many are self-imprisoned in 'Self-catraz', living non-authentic lives. This past summer I became a grandmother at the age of fifty-two. As I held Liam in my arms, I realized that his whole life lies before him as a clean slate. We have all tasted that freedom at one point or another and yet today many may feel incarcerated by past choices and current circumstances, living lives we neither imagined nor wanted. I'm here to say that that very same freedom is still ours for the taking.

Your journey may well take you down one of the roughest roads you'll ever walk, but the result will be worth any price paid. There is a price for freedom and the price is the courage and determination to change. As a child I remember playing many games of Monopoly. I always felt fortunate when I picked up the "Get Out of Jail Free" card. Life promises us no such card. Living free, authentic lives will always cost you something.

"There is no failure except in no longer trying. There is no defeat except from within, no insurmountable barrier except our own inherent weakness of purpose."

—Elbert Hubbard

To fear or not to fear—that is the question!

Yielding to fear will hold us back from the life we have imagined. Thank God for the many courageous men and women who have stepped out from behind the veil of fear and moved forward. Where would we be, had Christopher Columbus not had the courage to act on his belief that the world was round?

It's a given fact that everyday, thoughts of doubt and unbelief will assault our senses and attempt to immobilize us. Winning the battle will require us to incarcerate the negative thoughts rather than being incarcerated by them. Brace yourself! This is one battle that we will continue to fight all our lives.

Don't let fear keep you from acting on new choices—it's the only way to your new life. What I have discovered is that as you begin to move forward, fear dissipates and is replaced by a new sense of confidence and self-esteem.

> *"I always like to look on the optimistic side of life, but I am realistic enough to know that life is a complex matter."*
>
> —Walt Disney

Planning for a Jail Break?

Locate Yourself.

Ask yourself the following questions:

1. Do I find myself jealous of others when they meet with success?
2. Do I wish I were somewhere else, doing something else?
3. Do I feel that I don't make a difference in the lives of people around me?
4. Do I feel like there should be more to life?
5. Do I have trouble getting out of bed each day?

If you answered, "Yes" to even one question, let's start planning. It's time for a jailbreak that only you can mastermind.

Tired of the view from inside your cell? Steps to your personal Jail Break.

Step 1: Take an inventory of what landed you here

Are you blaming others for where you are and who you have become? Stop blame shifting. The prison break will never happen until you take ownership of the choices you have made and their consequences in your life. All our 'rap' sheets contain rejection, discouragement, disappointment, shame, loneliness, mistakes, regret or addictions, to name just a few. Are you struggling with the fact that what you "do" supports your current life style, fearful that pursuing "the dream" will cost too much?

No matter what it may look like there are no perfect people or perfect lives. People have become masters at concealing their weaknesses. Are you one of them? The truth is, you may be attempting to conceal "stuff" from others but are you really hiding "stuff" from yourself? Engaging in avoidance behavior regarding your current status will only continue to keep you from your dreams.

"Since no one is perfect it follows that all great deeds have been accomplished out of imperfection. Yet they were accomplished, somehow all the same."

—Lois McMaster Bujold

Step 2: Take a journey to the outside world; daydream your way out

You are unique. No one else living on this planet is quite like you. Far too many people are trying to be like someone else, meet someone else's expectation, etc. etc. Get the picture?

There have been times in my life when I felt like I was on a hamster wheel, simply going around and around but never getting anywhere different. Slow down; examine your life, allow yourself to daydream. I remember being reprimanded in my tenth grade math class, (not my strongest subject), for daydreaming. I promised myself that day that I would never stop dreaming, rather I would just choose the when and where more wisely.

The world is waiting for the authentic "You" to be revealed. The real "You" that you were created to be. As you take action the authentic life that is in your heart will manifest itself.

STEP 3: FINISHED DREAMING? NOW IT'S TIME FOR CHARACTER...

Courage:
"mental or moral strength to venture, persevere, and withstand danger, fear, or difficulty"

Determination:
"the quality of being resolute; firmness of purpose"

Persistence:
"firm or obstinate continuance in a course of action in spite of difficulty or opposition"

Dig deep. The pursuit of your dreams will take all the courage you can muster up. Interestingly enough, each person has enough courage to walk out his or her life. Courage is not the absence of fear, but rather continuing on in spite of it. We've all read stories where people have faced horrendous circumstances only to discover that they were stronger then they ever dreamed possible. The truth is acting on your dreams may well be one of the biggest fights of your life. It takes courage, persistence and determination to be different, to break the mold and reveal the new "You".

Do not be surprised that when you step out, the people around you may try to hold you back. They have been comfortable knowing you the way you were and when you change, they have to change their perception of you as well as themselves.

Persistence and determination are character traits so powerful that you must be sure you are applying them in the right direction. Your genuine gifts and talents will always lead you in the right direction and will be self-evident to others who have your best interest at heart. However, make sure you are applying these powerful traits to the genuine "You".

Consider the many thousands of American Idol contestants. Unfortunately many of the contestants think they possess star quality simply because they love to sing. I likewise love to sing but trust me, it will never be in front of an audience. Just because you love something doesn't mean that's what you're here to do.

My advice? Choose wisely and journey down the path that was created just for "You"

> *"I have learned that if one advances confidently in the direction of his dreams and endeavors to live the life he has imagined he will meet with success unexpected in common hours."*
> —Henry David Thoreau

Step 4: It's time to Take Action

> *"Inaction breeds doubt and fear. Action breeds confidence and courage. If you want to conquer fear, do not sit home and think about it. Go out and get busy."*
>
> —Dale Carnegie

Answer the following questions and you will be well on your way to having an escape plan.

The questions can include:

- "What am I afraid of?"
- "What's holding me back?"
- "What do I want out of my life?"
- "What are my passions, dreams, desires…?"

- "Why am I here, what's my purpose?"
- "What would living out my dream look and feel like?"
- "What changes do I have to make?"
- "Can I enlist someone to help, coach or mentor me in the areas where I need help?"
- "What are the steps?"
- "When do I start?"

"For true success ask yourself these four questions: Why? Why not? Why not me? Why not now?

—James Allan

My desire is that this chapter will encourage you to make the needed choices to facilitate your personal escape plan. I look forward to hearing your personal "Escape from Self-catraz" story as you live your new exciting authentic life on the "outside."

About the Author:

Diane L. Broos *is passionate about encouraging people of all ages to reach beyond where they are to where they want to be. Diane has applied this passion as an author, poet, personal coach, speaker, entrepreneur and management consultant. For helpful tips and information about writing a new escape plan for your life, free articles, audio podcasts, plus a free subscription to her newsletter, visit her website at* www.CreatedOne.com. *Contact her by email:* diane.broos@createdone.com, *telephone: 905-681-1400.*

CHAPTER 37

Take Care of Yourself First: Personal Success Habits that Can Give You A Better Life Too!

Dr. Cindy Brown, "The Business and Relationship Doctor"

At a very young age I learned to take care of myself if I wanted to feel good instead of feeling bad.

Picture this….

Sounds heard—Knock Knock, Knock Knock
—A little girl is heard crying outside her mother's closed bedroom door
—An adult female voice angrily—
"What do you want? Mommy's sleeping!"
—The little girl replies through her tears, and gasps, "I'm hungry mommy!"
—The mother indifferently and impatiently yelling from the bedroom "Ask your father, or get what you want in the kitchen. You can handle that yourself!"
—The child is heard stomping off, whimpering, and trying to comfort herself to prepare for her next journey... all alone.

As a child this was a scene played out repeatedly in my household. You see, I grew up in a family that looked 'normal' and healthy on the outside, like most in our neighborhood. You know—the one's where mom is home baking cookies and helps you with your homework, while dad works hard and is always smiling…..NOT!

If you looked behind the great big wooden doors of our house you saw a different picture.

You see, I grew up with a mother who was Bi-polar. When she was depressed, she locked herself away in her bedroom most hours of the day and left us kids to fend for ourselves.

She occasionally had good 'manic' days; those were the days she actually looked like a mother—on caffeine; cooking dinner; smiling; laughing; helping with homework; picking us up at school. The kind of mother others would see but never knew what was really going on behind the closed doors on the other days.

I liked the days she was manic, but I couldn't really count on them, as they were inconsistent. So I learned to count on myself mostly, which made me both happy and sad at times.

As you can see my childhood was a bit challenging at times. Mine was definitely not as bad as some of the early experiences I have heard my clients talk about in my private practice over the past 15 years, but nevertheless, it strengthened me to become the person I am today.

- I know how to take care of myself; figure out how to do things, like the main character on the T.V. show "MacGyver"
- I know how to read people emotionally to insure my safety and survival
- I notice when others are in need and what they need to feel better
- I know how to take care of myself first so I can take care of others after

I have learned over the years that many of us who have had very challenging childhoods actually become more successful when we use the very skills we learned and honed during our difficult situations.

The main skill I have learned and use daily, making me more successful everyday, is Take Care of Myself First. By using this skill I can be my best and be clear and available to others as an excellent Relationship Specialist, Executive Coach and Business Consultant.

Below is my 7 Step Strategy towards living a rich, self-sustaining, successful life that I have developed over the years:

1. Creating Daily Rituals: Know thyself—Take care of yourself:

There's a great saying *"Successful people do what unsuccessful people won't and don't do."* It is known that successful athletes and wealthy business people have particular daily habits and/or rituals they practice to make sure they perform the very best they can everyday.

I have many daily habits I perform each day that create a healthy foundation and a feeling of safety for me. I find that when I alter these drastically, I feel off balance and less creative and productive.

Each day I rise and start the morning being thankful for another day, my good health and prosperity. I light candles and do a special silent mediation and motivational reading. Then I do an emotional check in with my whole inner committee to see how I am feeling, thinking and being this day.

I find that self-reflection is a very important practice. I do it first thing in the morning and at night. I recommend creating your own daily practice of checking in to see how you feel, think, and what's unfinished. You can do this by writing, meditating or talking to yourself silently or out loud; I call this *Self Talk* (no, you're not crazy if you do this). I coach people on how to identify and work with their own inner committee so they know how and what to do to make it work successfully for them.

2. Begin and End Each Day with a Plan:

There's a famous quote that says, *"If you fail to plan, you plan to fail."* I always remind myself of this each day to motivate me to create my daily *trail map* so I can better navigate my day and accomplish my goals.

- I use a daily paper planning system because it is easily changed and I can scratch tasks off, plus I can print it and take it with me.
- I recommend preparing a separate sheet for each day's tasks. I use yellow paper as it stimulates my mind and catches my eye if it gets buried under my other paperwork.
- I look over my previous day's form and transfer any uncompleted tasks.
- I write a number next to each task to indicate priority (some people use letters A, B, C)
- I look at my project binder and see what tasks need to be completed for each project according to due dates and again priority (I also put a number next to these).
- I jot down time slots next to each task and sometimes use a kitchen timer to keep me on track.
- At the end of each day I look over what I have accomplished, observing my check marks and tasks I did not finish.
- I look at my calendar schedule for the next day so I can see what time I have available between clients, appointments etc.
- I start a new form for the next day transferring any uncompleted tasks.
- I have a little committee meeting with myself, celebrating my successes and coach myself to be more productive the next day…always with love and acceptance.

3. Exercise:

Releasing toxins and stress each day is an important practice for me and I've found in studying successful people that this is a #1 priority for them. I find it helps me maintain hormonal and chemical balance by giving me *Endorphins*; the natural anti-depressant or 'feel good' drug. I love the way I feel emotionally and physically after I workout.

I coach people on how to be successful with exercise and healthy eating as a lifestyle, not just a fad. It's part of my lifestyle and I love sharing with you what works for me!

4. Manage your Emotions. Talk yourself In or Out of Anything:

Did you know you have a very smart and proficient coach inside of you? You actually have a few coaches (your committee), some productive, some destructive. I teach people about their own unique committee and how to use them to become more successful and less destructive.

Use this committee to help you manage negative emotions; meet challenges; make decisions, and keep you motivated and moving towards your goals.

5. Communicate Effectively:

When you know how to communicate with others so they will listen, you can get your needs met better AND you stay out of upset more easily.

One step is to always start with the positive. Give a compliment or praise to allow people to be open to you and less defensive. Secondly, use "I" statements to communicate what you need to say. Never use "you" statements, because people equate that type of speaking with being talked 'down' to. No one enjoys being talked to like a child or feeling as if they are wrong. Also ask questions rather than making direct statements of blame.

6. Always Keep Learning:

Successful people keep on learning and growing. One of my favorite quotes is:

"Every time I learn something new it pushes some old stuff out of my brain."

—*Homer Simpson*

When you keep learning, you keep growing. And when you keep growing, you make your life richer and the world a better place by sharing your wisdom.

How do you keep learning? By reading, listening to CDs, radio, tele-seminars, hiring a coach, joining a Mastermind or Coaching Club, and attending live events.

7. Take care of your basic needs, so you can take care of others later:

Many of us learned somewhere that to get the attention and love we crave, we must sacrifice our own needs in order to take care of and please others. In doing so we deplete ourselves. We don't eat, sleep, or have enough personal time, so we get moody, angry, irritated, taking it out on others around us. This I find leads to an epidemic of anxiety, depression and mood disorders.

I take care of myself first by beginning every task or activity for another with a question I ask myself "What do I need to do for myself first in order to perform this task for another?" This *Self-Talk* shows me what I need, in order for me to be more available to others and not deplete myself.

Remember: In order to be the person you have never been you must do what you have never done before. Take care of yourself first so you can be a success. It's okay to get support to help you get there!

This is my story. I hope I have inspired and motivated you to pick your own success habits and perform them each day, so that these practices take you from *Whiner to Winner* just as they did me!

About the Author:

Dr. Cindy Brown, *a leading behavior specialist, executive coach, author, speaker and president of* Behavior, Relationship Institute Inc., *has helped 1000's of executives, individuals and couples improve their lives by examining and resolving their business and personal relationships issues. Her company's slogan is "A Healthier Way To Work and Live!" Please visit* www. SuccessfulRelationshipsNow.com *for your FREE Special Report and FREE Audio Class and* www.DrCindyBrownIntl.com *for your FREE copy of* Live Healthy, *her monthly ezine.*

CHAPTER 38

Thrive After Divorce:
6 Sure-Fire Principles to Take on
Any Challenge—And Win!

Carolyn B. Ellis

To the outsider, I looked like I had a picture-perfect life. Married to my high-school sweetheart and with a Masters degree from Harvard University, I enjoyed professional success in a number of ways. I'd worked on Wall Street, served as a senior government policy advisor and was a successful fundraiser. I was blessed with three healthy and happy children. How much better could life get?

Sure, it was challenging to recharge my batteries in between play dates, carpooling and meetings, but I thought juggling life's priorities was somehow character-building for me. Someday, life would get saner and my husband and I would live happily ever after.

My Wake-Up Call

Life didn't quite follow the script I had in mind. My marriage hit the rocks and in 2001 I was headed for a divorce. The divorce shattered every building block upon which I had constructed my life and self-concept. My emotional, parental, financial, legal, social and economic assumptions were all up for grabs. I hit bottom emotionally, gripped with fear and guilt that my divorce would permanently scar my young children.

One particular morning, I verbally exploded at my son for some trivial issue. This wasn't the first time I'd raised my voice as a parent. What was different, however, was the broken look I saw in his eyes. It shook me to my core. I heard a voice inside myself say, "That's it! You will do whatever it takes to heal yourself and stop taking it out on your kids. They deserve that!" I decided it wasn't good enough to simply "survive" or "get through" my divorce. For the sake of my children and myself, I chose to flourish and thrive instead.

I started the process of reinventing myself, training with some of the best transformational and business trainers in the world. The drive to thrive has sparked the birth of my new company, *Thrive After Divorce*. The company's mission is to empower people experiencing divorce around the globe to fearlessly create and express their highest potential. I've developed what I call the 'THRIVE' principles™, which can support you to create a life of passion, purpose and success.

The 'THRIVE' Principles™

The 'THRIVE' Principles™ have been fundamental to weathering any personal or professional challenge I've encountered. They are:
T – Trust
H – Honesty
R – Responsibility
I – Integrity
V – Vision
E – Expression

T – Trust

The first principle is to TRUST. Trust that you are made of the right stuff. You have every internal resource or skill that's needed to help you find your way through a problem. It's just a matter of learning how to access your own incredible talents.

Most importantly, you need to trust yourself. You are the world's best expert on you! Endlessly polling other people's opinions only leads to analysis paralysis. Trust that you will make mistakes and that you can learn from them. When in doubt, simply take a deep breath and check in with your intuition. Trust where your heart wants to lead you.

H – Honesty

It's so important to learn to be HONEST with yourself and with others. Without honesty, there can be no authenticity. When you can be real with yourself and with others, they can be real with you.

If you need help, be honest and ask for what you need. If you want to say no, be honest and decline. Often we say "yes" to a request just to be polite or "do the right thing", but then we carry out the task with resentment and procrastination! Honesty is critical for business and personal partnerships of all kinds. Satisfying, successful long-term relationships are built upon a foundation of honesty, not pretence.

R – Responsibility

The third principle is RESPONSIBILITY. As many great spiritual teachers tell us, we need to be 100% responsible for our current reality. Taking 100% responsibility puts you in the driver's seat of your life. Otherwise, you end up as the perpetual back-seat driver – always knowing better after the fact. You get to play the powerless victim, spending time and energy blaming others and making excuses for why you don't get what you say you want in life. When you harness the power of responsibility, you can affect change and take action to accomplish your goals.

Does that mean you're responsible for everything? No! You need to distinguish the things you're responsible for from the things that you're not. You are responsible for your thoughts, words and actions. Women seem particularly skilled at taking responsibility for the feelings and actions of others, while ignoring their responsibility to their own happiness and health. Before I truly understood the principle of responsibility, I was a great believer in being compassionate with other people by worrying about them. I ended up ignoring my own needs to the point where I let myself to become more of a doormat in personal and business relationships. Responsibility helps you set clear and healthy boundaries in business and personal relationships.

I – INTEGRITY

One of the most fundamental principles is INTEGRITY. Your word is incredibly powerful and sets the Universe in motion to align with your word. It's vital that you do what you say and say what you do. If you're not going to do something, declare that fact. Living in full integrity helps you to live "in the zone" where you'll find it effortless and magical to accomplish your goals.

Do you like to be with people who break promises to you? Well, that's what we do to ourselves when we compromise our integrity. When you're not practicing integrity, a part of your vital life force gets diverted and you drop out of the "zone" where things come to you effortlessly. As you expand your horizons, you have to keep raising the bar of your integrity.

In business I've found integrity to be an invaluable yardstick in choosing not only my business partners but my clients. Does someone call you when they say they will or follow-through on their actions? If they don't, chances are that lack of integrity pervades their life more broadly. You may be better off to not partner with those who do not share your commitment to integrity.

V – Vision

Whether you're creating a business, a relationship, a trim body or a new hobby, you must take the time to create an inspiring VISION for yourself. Without a vision, you don't have the big picture. Multi-tasking, information overload, overcrowded schedules and a high level of stress characterize life in the 21st century. It's easy to get caught up in battling daily brush fires, never feeling like you can get ahead.

Winston Churchill once said, "Never mistake the edge of your rut for the horizon." Articulating a vision defines your true horizon. Your vision should empower you and light you up from the inside. Holding a vision pulls you through the day-to-day challenges and keeps you in action towards your goals. Creating a successful business will take every ounce of energy, creativity and commitment that you have, so having a vision is absolutely critical.

I find it especially powerful to think of the people who will be served by my vision. There are tens of millions of divorced individuals in North America, with over 1 million children a year affected by divorce. As I develop my *Thrive After Divorce* business, I think of those people and see them better equipped and inspired to live happy, successful lives. Connecting to my vision of people thriving after divorce fuels me and keeps me going even when the going gets tough.

E – Expression

The final principle is EXPRESSION. Human beings have a huge spectrum of emotional expression. There's rage, sadness and fear at one end, and ecstasy and love at the other. Growing up I was very uncomfortable with anger so I did everything I could to never feel that way. I would avoid conflict at all costs or try to please other people. But as I capped my risk of feeling those strong negative emotions, I also limited my ability to fully feel the joyous positive emotions that live at the other end of the spectrum. It's living in our fullest expression of ourselves that we can feel fully alive.

It's been said that emotion is simply energy in motion. Bottling up your emotions is like putting psychic sludge into your system. Eventually you either shut down or you get backed up and explode. Expressing all of how I'm feeling is the best strategy I know for living full out and in the moment. You'll want to bring that energy and joy of life with you as you develop your business.

You Deserve to Thrive

Each of us is here because we have a unique talent or gift we bring to the world. Life is full of adversity and unexpected challenges along the way. Use the 'THRIVE' principles™ as the foundation for playing full out and delivering what you have to offer with passion, joy and ease!

About the Author:

Carolyn Ellis founded Thrive After Divorce, *a training and education company that empowers separated and divorced individuals. She is the author of* The 7 Pitfalls of Single Parenting: What to Avoid so Your Children Thrive After Divorce. *Carolyn teaches at the Institute for Integrative Coaching at John F. Kennedy University, founded by NY Times best-selling author, Debbie Ford. Visit* www.thriveafterdivorce.com *to get a free special report with success strategies for thriving after divorce.*

CHAPTER 39

How To Thrive, Not Just Survive, In Your Business: 5 Strategies to Create a Successful Business

Sandra P. Martini

You've most likely heard the statistics:

- Women are starting new businesses at three times the rate of men.
- 4 out of 5 new businesses fail each year.

Despite the odds, embarking on a new business, or choosing to grow an existing one, is a wonderful and exciting time!

I remember when I first started my own home business—"bright eyed and bushy-tailed" at being my own boss with no one to tell me what to do, when to do it, when to take a break, when to go on vacation, etc. Ahhh, the joy of it!

Once I started running my business from home however, reality set in very quickly!

- The days of commuting to and from a workplace with a defined work schedule (and paycheck) were gone.
- The days of being accountable to a "boss" were gone.
- The days of doing "home" stuff while at home and "work" stuff while at work were definitely gone!

Reality hit hard…I was now the owner, marketer, bookkeeper and service provider of a business let alone the personal stuff, and there were only 24 hours in a day!

I would feel guilty if the house was not spotless and I was spending too much time in the office (justified by "billable hours"). Or, conversely, if the house was clean and the laundry was done, but I wasn't making enough money.

Working 18 hour days with no end in sight, I refused to become one of the statistics and quickly realized there must be a better way.

Flash forward to today…I am a successful entrepreneur with a thriving business that I am passionate about. Doing what I love, I am able to take vacations and enjoy the life that I first envisioned when starting my own business (bunny slippers included).

The following strategies that have insured my success, and sanity:

1. PLAN FOR SUCCESS

The success of your business depends, in large part, on your mindset. Even before you become a business success, you need to think and act like one: thinking about the future, constantly learning and evolving, investing in yourself, modeling other successful people, building a strong team, writing goals and acting to achieve them, learning from failure—these are all things that successful people do on a daily basis.

This is part of the "Law of Attraction" which states that whatever you focus on, you will attract to you. If you are positive and moving forward in your life and your business, you will attract the same. If you are consistently focusing on success and wealth, that is what you will attract. If you are consistently focusing on money problems, you will attract more of the same.

By taking full responsibility for what is going on in your life—both the good and the bad—you will be able to control how you respond to it and that control will bring you success and happiness. Blaming others or focusing on the past will only work against you as it keeps you from moving forward.

2. Create a separate workspace that works for, not against, you

In deciding where you want to work, you need to first determine how you work.

Do you prefer a lot of space? Do you work with piles or does everything need its own file folder? Do you prefer a clear workspace with nothing except your current project or do you like to have all ongoing projects in sight? Determine how you work and where best suits your needs.

Whether you take over a spare bedroom, a corner of the basement or the dining room table be sure that you have a space that is yours just for working. Doing so will allow you to more easily switch into business mode when you sit down.

In setting up your office, don't run out and buy every gadget known to woman. It's tempting to get the best of everything right off the bat—resist the urge! There's no reason to go into debt for items you will never use.

Get the basics and add things when there is a need. For my purposes, the basics are: a good laptop, a multi-line telephone with speakerphone and mute, a color laser printer, a scanner and a separate hard fax machine (in addition to my electronic fax account). What you need will depend on what your business is and how you work with your clients.

3. Do what you do best and know when to say "when"

I love what I do and draw a lot of energy from it. That said, be sure you set limits both on what you do and on how long you spend working each day so as not to drain yourself.

My workday typically starts around 8am and I go until lunch when I take a break, grab the dogs and go for a walk. Once back, I work for a few more hours and then do a final check of everything in the evening. This schedule works well for me. You need to find one that works for you—if you have children, your prime workday may be while they are at school or after they've gone to bed. It's important to work while you are most productive rather than forcing yourself to conform to a 9am to 5pm schedule.

Even when working your perfect schedule, working from home can lead to a sense of isolation and the feeling that you need to do everything yourself. You don't. It's important that you build a team to help build your business—I have a coach, a financial advisor and a prepaid legal contract all ready to support me in reaching the next level.

Focus on those things that you do best—the reasons why you chose to go into business for yourself—and outsource or automate the rest. A virtual assistant can help you with all those tasks that you shouldn't be spending time on. It is better for your business to hire someone, say to do the books, than it is for you to spend X hours trying to figure it out when you could be marketing your business or working directly with your clients.

Whenever possible, set up your systems such that regular tasks are as automated as possible. Do you have an evergreen (i.e. never changing, same for everyone) welcome email that you send all your new clients? If so, set up an autoresponder.

Need to keep track of projects and have updates automatically sent to clients? Use an Intranet solution such as WebOffice. Need to explain something "in person" to a potential client? Use a webinar. Using technology to your advantage will allow you to focus on those things that you enjoy and push you forward.

4. BE YOURSELF...AS UNIQUE AS SHE IS

Your business is an extension of you and you want to insure that it comes through in everything you do. I have long been known by my friends and family as the one who sends cards. I send cards for happy occasions, for sad occasions and then just for no reason at all. I've incorporated this "trait" into my marketing plan such that I send my clients the usual holiday cards (which I'm sure get buried with everyone else's) and then a few extra: a Thanksgiving Day card to thank them for their business, a late January card to see how they are doing with all those New Year's resolutions and a card for the beginning of spring just "because". It doesn't cost much and adds yet another layer to my marketing while being true to what I enjoy.

Try to find little ways to incorporate your personality into everything you do. The more true you are to yourself, the more you will attract the right clients—people with whom you mesh and who you look forward to working with.

5. Get out of the office

As you work on your marketing plan, take care of your clients and generally build your business, it's easy to forget the outside world exists.

Be sure you get out of your home office (and your pj's) at least once a week. Go anywhere there are people: the gym, a favorite coffee shop, networking events, out with friends, etc. You'll get far more ideas by getting out and about and mixing with people.

I also make it a point to go on a business retreat at least once a year. I usually plan my retreat in late summer—it's late enough in the current year to have a good idea of how the year is progressing and yet still have enough time to make changes if necessary. I take a few critical tools and go somewhere for a few days where I can sit and reflect on my business as a business, with its successes and opportunities.

With a little planning, you can create a successful business that reflects you and all that you love.

About the Author:

Sandra Martini *teaches small business owners how to create more success in their business while maintaining their sanity and having fun. Clients range from entrepreneurs, coaches, and virtual assistants to Feng Shui practitioners and real estate investors. For more information and to receive the FREE special report,* 7 Wealth-Building Secrets of Successful Entrepreneurs, *go to* www.thevirtualsolution.com.

CHAPTER 40

Escape The Pace, Life's Not a Race: Slowing Down is the Key to Success at Work and Home

Lisa Rickwood

"On the keyboard of life, always have one finger on the escape key."
—Anonymous

A Common Societal Belief:

Over 20 years ago, I never dreamed I'd be where I am today—teaching others about the importance of slowing down. In fact, my mantra went like this: "I'll slow down when I'm dead."

I remember deducing in grade 12 that if you sleep eight hours a day and live to the ripe old age of 90, you've slept 30 years of your life. "What a waste," I thought. "I have much too much to do to sleep that much."

I continued this philosophy through my 20s and seemed puzzled by my constant health problems, colds and other illnesses. I didn't realize the restorative power of sleep or 'escaping the pace' until a major event rocked my world. This occurred in my 30s—a time when most of us hopefully get wiser about life. My story goes like this:

Imagine you've just cinched a deal with your life partner to buy a 42 year-old high-end menswear store during a recession, and, you don't know anything about menswear. How's that for stress?

Now, imagine you hire a wonderful older gentleman to help with the Christmas rush and this beautiful man collapses on his fourth day of work; he dies of a heart attack right in front of you. How would you feel? To make matters worse, that same day you have to attend the unveiling of your partner's oil painting for a 15th wedding anniversary and pretend everything is fine. Every time you talk to a guest at the party, your brain rewinds to the events earlier in the day. It takes every ounce of strength for you to stay at the celebration and fake happiness.

During this time in 1999, I was working six days a week and caring for my two young sons, ages two and six. I wasn't healthy for more than two weeks that year. I kept getting rare viruses and fell into a depression. I felt trapped, hopelessly burnt out, and desperate. I knew there had to be a better way to live. Somehow in my darkest hour, I realized life was precious and too much time was wasted being miserable and stressed. I knew I couldn't change my circumstance but could change my attitude if I wanted to be there for my husband and my sons.

A SIMPLE SOLUTION:

I lacked money for counseling so I read numerous books about stress reduction, relaxing, and slowing down. Eventually I interviewed people, wrote articles and began recording my findings that later became my book, *Escape The Pace*. The greatest piece of advice that came from years of research was this: *just slow down, if only for a moment.*

In a complex world, a simple solution to a growing epidemic seems too easy but that's just what it is—easy…at least after a while.

If people think slowing down means making less money, not working hard and not being successful, then they've missed the boat. Escaping the pace is about taking a mini holiday amidst the chaos and busyness of life. Why one would ask? The answer is really quite simple—to have more energy to deal effectively with any situation that may arise.

We are a nation that prides itself on workaholism and productivity. We're not comfortable with slowing down; we feel guilty when we take a break. We're so conditioned to multi-tasking, bragging about our accomplishments and 'looking busy'. We also avoid slowing down because it means we have to face issues in our lives we don't like.

How many times have you returned home to an empty house and found yourself turning on the television, computer or stereo to eliminate the silence? The silence most likely bothered you because you were forced to slow down, thus you had time to think about your day, your actions—the bigger picture. As soon as you felt uncomfortable, you picked up the pace and started cleaning, watching television or getting involved in some other distracting activity.

We think we're doing ourselves a favor by running ourselves ragged, but we're not helping our lives. You know what happens when you burn the candle at both ends? The flames eventually meet in the middle and that candle is incinerated.

This philosophy of always having to be busy or 'look busy' leaves us feeling exhausted, disconnected and frustrated—not the prerequisites for building an amazing life.

The key to a fantastic life is to escape the pace once in a while. Everything in nature relaxes, why should we be any different?

I have a beautiful peach tree that grows against the back of my house. In the first week of August, the tree's branches are laden with large yellow, pink and red sweet fruit that's warm to the touch.

This tree doesn't yield fruit every year. Instead, it produces a large amount of fruit every second year; the tree grows and rebuilds itself during the lean years. Everything in nature is like this—except mankind.

Living in the moment, relaxing or taking a break, is about reclaiming your personal power and honoring the only thing we can't get more of—time. In a world that constantly pulls us out of ourselves, this is critical and unselfish. This gives us power to excel in the world and allows us to decide if the path we're on is appropriate or if we need to make changes. You can't change what you don't acknowledge and if you don't have time to pay attention, you lose precious time doing things that don't add to your life.

Temporarily escaping the pace is like recharging your laptop or cell phone—they work better when they're fully charged. So will you.

Think back to when you took a power nap, had a good night's sleep, worked out at the gym or went on a long hike. Did these activities seem like a waste of time? No. In fact, you probably felt energized and had energy to do more things once you returned from that activity

It doesn't matter whether you take 10 minutes or one day to recharge, relax, have fun or escape—what matters is that you do it every day. Just give yourself permission.

What can you do during these 'escape' times? You should participate in anything that takes you away from work or errands. You might walk your dog, practice yoga, jog, lift weights, stare into space, read, write—it doesn't matter what it is, it just needs to be something that makes you happy, takes you away from responsibilities and makes you feel energized.

If you're stressed and time-starved and question how you can possibly find time for yourself, try this one idea—eliminate one thing each day or week that doesn't have to be done and replace it with something you enjoy.

Your passion can take you five minutes or a day—it doesn't matter. It only matters that you make space in your life to slow down.

What's the point? When you slow down, you have time to appreciate the moment, think about things you're working on or striving for, take time to really listen to friends and family, and discover ways to improve ongoing challenges—something that never happens when you're constantly rushing from one place to another, one task to another.

Remember that it takes 30 days for something to become a habit so if you find yourself forgetting or seeming to lack time to implement escaping, don't beat yourself up—there's always tomorrow.

"After all, life is not a race."

About the Author:

Lisa Rickwood, *BFA, CPCC, is an accomplished visual artist, speaker, work/life coach and author of* Escape The Pace: 100 Fun and Easy Ways to Slow Down and Enjoy Your Life. *Her articles have appeared in newspapers across North America, and she has been interviewed by U.S. Magazine, First For Women, and written for Woman's World. She's been featured in numerous books and television interviews. You can reach Lisa at:* info@escapethepace.com, www.escapethepace.com *or phone: 250-753-4271 or 250-753-4100.*

CHAPTER 41

Back from Betrayal

SHERI ROWLAND

Have you ever been betrayed, accused or threatened? I have and here's how I survived.

Over a year ago I decided that I wanted to enlarge my coaching practice to include teaching and writing. I'd always loved writing and had been journaling for 20+ years and felt I had something to share with others. Plus it would provide more introductions to potential clients.

Even as scared as I was to put myself out into the world in such a big way, I registered for a Teleclass to help me create and market my product. During that 90 day Teleclass I created an eBook, workbook and audio addressing men and women's weight issues using a variety of writing exercises, visualizations, affirmations and a myriad of energy exercises and techniques.

I invited others to joint venture with me in my campaign. Everything was progressing along nicely when out of the blue, I was wrongly accused of copying another writer's materials from her book; threatened for monetary compensation to rectify it; had to hire an attorney, and had to stop my products from going into the marketplace. Over the next 9 months I endured nasty, repulsive and disgusting emails from this woman. Do you think I would have sent my eBook to her if I had copied her work? Needless to say, I shut down. I squandered away a lot of my energy over what her opinion was of me, and this situation attacked me at my very core.

I shut down everything. My eBook, campaigns, sales letters, my website and even myself. This sucked the life force out of me and took the wind out of my sails. I went in to a place of sheer panic and started questioning everything about my new products, and even myself. I was experiencing such a vast sea of emotions and feelings that I had to search for what was the truth. Had I copied anyone's work? Where did I get the affirmation and the opening line for my chapter title? The affirmation was one that I had written in my journal 7 years ago. The line? Who knows? But I had never seen this woman's book, so I knew I had not copied her work.

To recover from this traumatic event I started treating myself with kindness and self care. I started walking around the lake in front of my home several times a day. Being out in nature seemed to soothe and comfort me. I was doing energy techniques to alleviate my fears, and using essential oils such as Peace and Calming and Joy. Digging in the dirt and cutting fresh wild flowers for my house seemed to ground me. I was lighting candles, incense and saging the house. Praying. I was journaling and writing down my thoughts and feelings, my concerns and singing. Yes, singing. Did you know that you cannot think and sing at the same time?

Rather than living in fear and allowing my thoughts to take me to what might happen next week, next month or further on, I knew I needed to stay in the present moment. I believe in the importance of the Law of Attraction; that I would attract into my experience that with which I am in vibrational resonance with. So rather than listen to my thoughts, which did not make any sense at the time, it was best that I just sing. I also needed to stay in the present moment. I would sit quietly, close my eyes, and center my thoughts on my breathing and on my heart center—that space in the center of your chest. As thoughts would come into my mind, I would acknowledge them, but then let them pass on by like floating clouds.

I was also talking about this incident to death. At the time I was in various professional relationships with some of the top coaches in the country. I was conversing with them, getting feedback on how to handle this situation, and seeing if they had a take on the circumstances. I talked with numerous colleagues and my trusted attorney. They all assured me that I was in the right—that this gal did not have solid ground to stand on.

I knew this in my heart but my head was saying something else. I had to get my head and my heart on the same playing field. My heart and my head were at 'war' with each other constantly. At times, I felt schizophrenic!

I don't write about all this so that you can take sides or even know about the situation. I write about it so that you can see what I did to personally survive

this ordeal and mostly to show you what I learned and what techniques worked to help me through this situation.

It forced me to search deep inside myself to find out who I really was and what I was made of. It forced me to look at both my internal and external support systems. After numerous journal entries, I began to know again that I lived in integrity—that I was an honest person. I was a loving and caring mother, a good friend and a thoughtful daughter. I was a great counselor and a super coach.

I also used Emotional Freedom, Tapas Acupuncture Techniques and Body Talk. I would look around me and connect with nature, the majesty of the mountains, the trees, the sheer beauty that surrounded me. I would find God, the Universe, my Higher Self, Mother Earth or a Higher Power in all that I saw. I would connect with the God that created all this wonder around me and know in my heart that He/She made me too. I knew that I was not alone and that this Power that is greater than me was with me throughout this whole ordeal. It seemed that the more faith that I had, the more ease and acceptance I had with the situation. I made a decision everyday to not take those negative thoughts with me into my bedroom. I journaled every morning and every evening so that I would go to bed clear of any negative thoughts and sleep well. I also soaked in bubble baths that calmed and hushed my thoughts and fears. I increased my vitamins, ate healthier than before and increased my exercise levels.

My head gave me the power to change my thoughts, my attitudes, my choices, my behaviors, and my actions, while my heart allowed me to change my feelings and my emotions. Until I could get my head (which was my thoughts and actions), right, I had no power. And until I got my heart (which was my feelings), right, I could not connect with my soul. My head was my power and my heart was my soul. Somehow I had to get my head and heart on the same playing field in order to create balance in my life once again.

Sometimes painful situations can cause you to find a part of you that you did not know existed. The part of you that has survived many difficult situations and continues to thrive. The part of you that is the very best of you.

I came to realize that people who try to intimidate, blackmail, and issue threats against others, actually live in a world of scarcity and lack. I had to learn to forgive her because that is where she is coming from. I knew in my heart that I come from a place of abundance and that I did not need to feel threatened.

The positives that came from this experience is that I am incorporating the steps that I took to process and survive this ordeal to come out a much stronger and powerful woman into my new business. I believe that that is why this incident showed up in my life at that time—so that I could perfect my eBook, workbook and audio products. To create a whole new series around living in integrity and honesty and the steps to help maintain your energy and shift your limiting beliefs about yourself and others. I believe in looking for the positive in everything and that is what I choose to continue to focus on.

Would you please take time to consider the following?

What situation has taken the fire out of your soul?

To whom and where have you given away your power?

What steps do you need to take in order to work through this issue?

Is there someone that you need to forgive?

I encourage you to take the first steps to working through whatever is holding you back. Staying connected and in balance with your power and your soul is where your true power lies!

Sometimes negative events like this happen to get us to re-evaluate our life—to grow and look within ourselves to become a much stronger person. I know today that my relationship with myself shows the quality of love that shines in my work. After a year now, I am a much stronger, focused woman in my personal and professional life. I have become inspired to create again—to create products, eBooks, a new practice, and a new me!

I have a new fire in my soul to be 'present' in today. 'Present' in my life!

About the Author:

Sheri Rowland, *MA is a motivated, passionate Life Transitions Coach. Using her 20 years of coaching/counseling experience and eclectic background, she assists her clients through natural and unexpected passages, ultimately guiding them to a life filled with joy, passion and fun. Sign up for her FREE monthly ezine offering tips, insights and challenging steps to help move you forward in life. Visit* www.sherirowland.com *for information on coaching sessions for individuals/groups or contact her at* sheri@sherirowland.com.

CHAPTER 42

Embracing Chaos with Grace: Balancing the Worlds of Modern Mommy and Money Maven

Elizabeth Potts Weinstein, JD, CFP®

I do not dispense financial and legal advice from an upper floor of a high-rise, wood paneled office, leaning from an antique leather chair over a mahogany conference table. My advice is dispensed while a toddler is yanking on my sweater, with Dora the Explorer blaring in the background, while I pick cracker crumbs off client forms and use a laptop with a missing 'k' key. The 21 months I have simultaneously run a startup company while caring for my daughter, Grace, have been a gift—even when we were drowning in chaos.

THE ADVENTURE BEGINS

Unlike many work-at-home moms, I did not start my company in response to having a child. I was proactive. I knew that 70 hour work weeks in a boring (yet allegedly successful and lucrative), legal career was not going to jive with my priorities when my husband and I wanted to start a family. Even more, I wanted to help regular people change their lives—and create something of my own. So I walked away and hung my virtual shingle on the web.

The startup of my business was slow at first, until the summer of 2004 when I was featured in the local newspaper. I went from one call a week to 12 calls a day. I was caught in the momentum of my growing business, working 10 hours a day and loving it—the financial planning firm was my 'baby'.

And then I got pregnant. Yes, it was sort of planned, but we had thought we would wait until my business was more established. But the powers that be had something else in mind for us. Our Master Plan was for me to take 6 weeks off upon the birth of the baby, hire a nanny part time for a few months, then go back to my business full-time, with the baby either in daycare or with a full-time nanny. In the spring, Grace was born (and God laughed).

Lesson #1: You Must Fill Yourself First

A few days after she was born, I was intoxicated with Grace. I held her almost 24 hours a day. I watched her sleep, worried over her feedings, and demonstrated all her toys. Those first few weeks, I was energized by her newness (or perhaps from the birth and nursing hormones). But Grace was a bottomless pit of need, and I was not able to constantly fill it by myself.

Grace, to this day, needs constant motion. Before she was able to crawl or walk, she wanted that motion to be provided by the grown ups in her life, 24-hours a day. She would deconstruct if left to her own devices—as if her brain was unable to process the world without some motion to occupy part of her mind. A few months of this, and I was getting used up.

When her new part-time nanny arrived, I was oppressed with guilt. How could I give my baby to a stranger and dare to run a business? We could live off of my husband's salary. Was my business just a selfish conceit? Should I be a stay-at-home mom for a few years and start my business up again when she goes off to school?

By the end of the day of nanny care, I already knew I had made the right decision. I was able to fill my needs by living in the world of adults—reading emails, solving problems, learning new ideas, eating a civilized business lunch—such that when Grace returned, I was ready, able, and overjoyed to give to her again. By taking care of myself first, Grace is no longer a drain. She is my joy.

Lesson #2: Don't Listen to What You "Should" Do. Trust Yourself & Trust Your Baby

As Grace made the transition from babyhood to toddlerhood, life became much more complicated. My active toddler would no longer be amused by playing in a jumper seat while I answered email. No, she wanted to cruise the house for trouble, climb the furniture, chase the cat while screaming, append my notes with her Crayola commentary, and disassemble my stapler.

How could I get anything done outside of my part-time nanny hours? Should I put Grace in full-time nanny or day care? Does she need more stimulation than I can provide? Should I reduce my client workload and stop expanding my business?

Ignoring what "they" say about TV for kids under 2, I purposely sat down with Grace and indoctrinated her to Elmo and Dora. After a few sessions she was a certified convert, and started learning the words to songs, dancing to the music, and pointing out the paraphernalia at Target.

Did Grace turn from a lean, smart, rambunctious toddler to a chubby, lazy, couch potato? Was she unable to understand reality because she was exposed to a fast-moving, short-segment virtual world, full of impossible situations and furry monsters?

Oh, please. Of course not!. For a few weeks she was a bit of an addict, demanding her new friends every time she was present in the living room. But now, it is just one more way for her to learn. Typically, she only has one eye on the TV—she's also chasing the cat, sorting trucks, and undressing a doll. Given the choice, she would much rather throw rocks off the slide or dance around with mommy, than watch the big black box.

By using television as another tool, I am able to get a few more things done, expose Grace to different stimulation and information—yet spend quality, dedicated 1:1 time enjoying my daughter. Instead of blindly following someone else's rules, I trust myself and my daughter to find the balance that is right for us.

Lesson #3: Embrace the Chaos

When Grace was 1 ½ we went without childcare for a few weeks, while our nanny was on leave. I reserved just one day of backup daycare each week through my husband's work, for client meetings—and planned to get all the work done while taking care of Grace... somehow.

That month was a struggle. Grace wanted attention and mommy was overwhelmed. I had just started teaching a teleclass, adding another 5+ hours per week to my already-impossible workload. I also had the wonderful problem of more clients—and did not have time for both meetings and work in one day of childcare each week. But I pressed on, counting down the days until our nanny returned from leave.

One particular Tuesday we learned the number one detriment to daycare. That Monday, Grace had a booster shot and had felt a bit fussy that afternoon. Tuesday morning, she woke up with a 103 degree fever. Oh. No. No daycare allowed for the feverish, no matter that the culprit was a vaccination.

What to do? I had two prospect appointments that day, a client project due in two days, two classes to teach and class notes to finish. Should I douse her up with Motrin and hope the daycare does not notice? Should I call a service for a sick-care nanny? What will my clients say if I cancel at the last minute? Am I no longer a professional and am I being flaky if I call in baby-sick?

My baby needed me, so I emailed my clients, prospects, and class students to reschedule the appointments and classes. But I resented it. I resented Grace for being sick. I resented my husband for going to work. I resented the world for providing no easy solution. Why was I burdened with this baby in the supposedly modern age of women's lib? During her nap that afternoon, Grace woke fitfully, still very tired but too feverish to be comfortable. I swooped her up in my arms and we cuddled on the sofa. Immediately upon resting her head on my chest, feeling the beat of my heart, Grace became peaceful, and went back to sleep. I watched her and drank her up. Her sweaty hair, curling under on her neck, her damp pj's, her rosy cheeks, her perfect, blemish-free skin, that unnamable baby-smell emanating from her hair—was there anything in the world more beautiful?

Screw clients, business, and expectations of being a modern woman. I am the world to Grace, the most important thing in her life right now, and she is my #1 priority. There is nothing that's more fulfilling than nurturing her into the woman she will become. She is my ultimate project, and even though I may change the world through my company, growing Grace is my most important endeavor.

Instead of fighting the unpredictability, I now embrace the challenge. Running a business and raising my daughter, I'm more efficient, empathetic, flexible, and creative. Everyday as I type on my computer with Grace squirming in my lap, I know that I have been blessed with a life uniquely designed to stimulate me and grow me into the woman that I am destined to become—both as Grace's mommy, and as an entrepreneur.

About the Author

Elizabeth Potts Weinstein, *JD, CFP® is passionate about helping young professional women achieve their biggest life goals through strategic financial planning, coaching, and education. Elizabeth is the creator of The Wealth Spa™, a revolutionary program to empower women to makeover their finances and transform their lives. Contact Elizabeth at* planning@thewealthspa.com, *800-752-3592, or* www.thewealthspa.com. *To learn more about how to stop money stress and achieve your goals, visit* www.prosperezine.com *and receive a free Special Report.*

CHAPTER 43

How to Quit Your Job and Get a Life — The Four Things You Need to Know to Change Course Fast

VALERIE YOUNG

For seven years I commuted 90 miles a day to a high-stress corporate job. It was a job that paid the bills but did not feed my spirit. Then one day I got a painful wake up call. My mother died unexpectedly of a heart attack at age 61. She died just five months before her much-awaited retirement. It was a sorrowful reminder that life really is too short and precious to defer something as important as our dreams and that "someday" doesn't always come.

Five months later I'd accepted a position at a smaller company with half the commute. Life was good… or so I thought. Before long the perfect job turned out to be the job from hell. That's when it hit me...

I Didn't Need a New Job—I Needed a New Life!

What I really wanted was a life with more balance, work I could feel passionate about, and the ability to control my own life and time. That's the day I decided to follow my bliss.

It sounds cliché, but small steps really do add up. Two years after my Mom died I left the corporate world forever. Today I sit in my sun-filled office with a view of the distant hills. I work at what

I want, how I want, and when I want. Once I'd taken the leap, I set out to help others reach "the other side." In the process I learned there are four things you need to know to quit your job and get a life.

1. KNOW WHAT YOU WANT

No one in their right mind would deliberately sign up for a life of commuter traffic, cubicles, or office politics. We just end up with whatever life comes with the job. But what if it was the other way around? What if your life was the engine that drove the career train?

My Life-First, Work-Second Approach to Career Planning™ starts with the question, "What do I want my life to look like?" Once you figure out what you want your life to look like then you can come up with ways to generate income that will allow you to have as much of that life as possible.

Your vision of your ideal life also serves as a screening device for your career choices. For example, if you know that your idea of heaven-on-earth would be spending spring in Italy, then it's a matter of coming up with one or more income streams that are portable or location specific. Making sure your work passes the "Life Test" helps you avoid the career equivalent of changing deck chairs on the Titanic.

What about you? Would you love to work a four-day work week or spend the morning puttering in your garden? Do you want to hire someone to handle all of the "administrivia" of your business? Or perhaps you simply want to work at home so you can spend more time with your family.

As you create your mental picture, think about how much money you want to earn. Take whatever figure came to mind and double it. Now triple it. Now take a deep breath, smile and keep going.

Bonus Tip: When you're stuck in 'job jail' it's easy to dwell on what you *don't* want. But devoting five minutes a day to visualizing the "good life" will move you far closer to your dream than that hour you spent dwelling on that annoying co-worker.

2. Know What You Have

"Know what you have" speaks to the need to tune into your unique gifts and interests, or in other words, what do you really love to do? Notice I didn't ask you what you're *good* at. Your skills or previous experience may reveal little about what you would be truly happy doing. I'm good at typing and mowing the lawn, but that doesn't mean I want do either for a living!

Instead, think about the kinds of things you really love. Is it gardening? Surfing the Web? Giving advice? Sports talk? Shopping for bargains? Home decorating? Dogs? Consider compliments you receive. Others often recognize your gifts before you do!

Think, too, about "assets" you have or could acquire. For example, owning rental property or timesharing a boat could supplement your current salary during your transition to self-employment. An asset might also take the form of intellectual property you can turn into a product or service, like massaging something you've written previously into an eBook or parlaying some "insider" knowledge into a consulting practice.

A final thought: For hundreds of millions of impoverished people around the world life is about survival, not fulfillment. "Knowing what you have" also means recognizing the incredible luxury you and I have to pursue satisfying work.

3. Know Who Wants What You Have

Next ask yourself, "Who wants what I have?" This is the person or organization that is going to write you a check, enter their credit card, give you a contract, or otherwise pay you for the gifts and interests you just identified.

In addition to prospective customers and clients, expand your thinking to include potential sponsors, collaborators, partners, and referrers. Take professional organizer Barbara Perman. Her company, *Moving Mentor*, helps seniors transition from life-long homes into assisted living. Who wants what Barbara has?

In addition to seniors and their adult children, there are the assisted living communities themselves and referral sources like gerontologists, visiting nurses, and senior centers. Don't forget realtors, antique appraisers, auction houses, vintage clothing and jewelry stores, and eBay sellers.

But that's not all. Local companies might want to add Barbara's services to their employee benefit package. Plus she could create a "business in a box" to train others interested in starting a similar business in their area. From here Barbara could develop joint partnerships with Web sites like mine that promote reputable home-based business opportunities to aspiring entrepreneurs.

Bonus Tip: Just because you're a one or two person operation, don't be afraid to tap corporate sponsors. When *Major in Success* author Patrick Combs wanted to grow his speaking business he partnered with Visa to sponsor a national speaking tour.

4. KNOW HOW TO SUCCEED—FASTER!

Making any significant work/life change takes time. That said, there are ways you can change course faster: Become an "Opportunity Analyst"

Opportunities for income streams are all around you. Finding creative alternatives to having a job requires learning to become an "Opportunity Analyst." There are five places to look for income generating ideas, one of these is trends. The growing aging population led one enterprising Canadian to start a driving service for senior citizens called Driving Miss Daisy. The trend toward aimless college graduates moving home with their parents presents an opportunity to offer life and career coaching for college grads.

Perhaps the easiest place to look for business ideas is your own personal experience. As an intellectually insecure 24-year-old doctoral candidate I was sure it was just a matter of time before I would be "found out." I soon learned I was not alone. Like a lot of opportunities, this one came disguised as a problem. So many people suffer from the so-called Impostor Syndrome that I've used my experience as a "recovering impostor" to speak on the subject to over 30,000 people at such diverse organizations as Daimler Chrysler, Harvard, and American Women in Radio and Television.

PRACTICE THE ART OF WINGING IT

Before they dare hang out their shingle or present themselves as an authority most women mistakenly believe they need to know 150 percent, have 20 years experience—or both! But if you're starting a new business you may not have a track record. That means from time you'll need to "fake it 'til you make it."

For example, Nightline's Ted Koppel was asked by a Newsweek reporter if he ever felt like he "didn't know enough about a subject to ask the tough questions." Koppel replied:

"No. When I can, I'd rather go into a program knowing as much as possible about the subject, but I don't consider it a handicap [when] I know next to nothing." What he said next forever changed my thinking. "[I figure I can]…pick up enough information in a short period of time to be able to bullshit my way with the best of them."

Clearly a respected journalist like Ted Koppel is no "bullshit artist." What Koppel was talking about is the art of winging it. Don't like the idea of faking it? Then substitute words like improvising, thinking on your feet, chutzpah! Start viewing "winging it" not as proof of your ineptness but as the skill that it is.

Life is too short not to follow your dreams. Charles Handy put it well when he said, "For the first time in the human experience, we have a chance to shape our work to suit the way we want to live instead of always living to fit in with our work... We would be mad to miss the chance."

About the Author:

Dreamer in Residence, **Valerie Young**, *is an expert on turning interests into income and making the leap to self-employment. She's been featured in The Wall Street Journal, Entrepreneur, Inc., USA Weekend, Self, Kiplinger's, Glamour, Redbook, Cosmopolitan, The Chicago Tribune, Woman's Day and online at MSN, iVillage, and CareerBuilder. Sign up for free breakthrough success tips, inspiring stories, and practical resources to help you find your life mission and live it at* www.ChangingCourse.com/ezine *or visit* www.ChangingCourse.com.

ABOUT ALEXANDRIA K. BROWN

The stories in this book were compiled by entrepreneur and million-dollar marketing and success coach Alexandria K. Brown.

A former New York ad-agency employee, Ali left to form her own business (with a very slow start).

After finally mastering the marketing basics, she found the exact online formula needed to catapult herself to being the authority in her newfound niche of ezine publishing. (You may have heard her referred to as "The Ezine Queen.")

Her courses and coaching have since taught thousands of small business owners how to use the Internet and simple marketing systems to become well-known, work less, have more fun in their business, and… make a lot more money!

Ali has worked with clients including New York Times Digital, Adweek Magazines, Scholastic Books, and Dun & Bradstreet, but her passion lies in showing entrepreneurs how to create consistent streams of online income using their expertise and personality.

More than 350 small business owners are members of her Marketing & Motivation Mastermind program, receiving Ali's personal coaching by Internet, phone, fax, and live in person. (To learn more about joining this exceptional group of entrepreneurs, see the following page.)

Ali has been sponsored as a speaker by Microsoft, interviewed by *The Wall Street Journal,* and has been featured in *Entrepreneur Magazine* and countless marketing books including *Confessions of Shameless Internet Promoters*. A dynamic speaker whose presentation style "rocks the house," Ali has spoken at large events hosted by marketing and motivational geniuses Dan Kennedy, Mark Victor Hansen, and others, all around the world from the United States to Australia.

Now a converted California girl, Ali lives on the beach in Marina del Rey with her cat Francine and "Scooter", her New Beetle Convertible. You may contact Alexandria at:

ALEXANDRIA K. BROWN
AKB Communications Inc.
578 Washington Blvd. Ste. 130
Marina del Rey, CA 90292
877-510-2215 phone
877-742-8056 fax
info@AlexandriaBrown.com
www.AlexandriaBrown.com

Enjoy 3 FREE MONTHS in
Alexandria K. Brown's
Marketing & Motivation Mastermind

Besides having some amazing stories to share, all of the authors in this book are also part of Alexandria Brown's *Marketing & Motivation Mastermind*. This stellar group of 450+ likeminded entrepreneurs focuses on marketing & sales success, wealth building, personal fulfillment, and *designing your business to create an extraordinary life™*.

Ali would like tos offer you a **FREE 3-month trial membership** in her Mastermind just for reading this book! As a Mastermind Member, you'll enjoy:

- **Monthly LIVE phone calls** with Ali and her hand-picked expert guests, covering important business and success strategies that will inspire you, increase your sales, help you work less, and make you more money!
- **Online digital recordings** and **written transcripts** of each and every call
- **CD recordings** and bonus "hot sheets" of every call mailed to you direct
- Private access to our exclusive **Mastermind Online Forum** to network, get questions answered, and promote yourself and your business
- Ali's **"Million Dollar Resource Rolodex"**, featuring the tried and proven marketing and business resources Ali and her clients use

... and even more surprises!

This offer is only good for a limited time, so please don't miss out. Learn more now about this exclusive, life-changing program, and claim your *FREE 3-month trial membership* at:

www.AlexandriaBrownMastermind.com